# NOW YOU KNOW

## MORE

# The Book of Answers
# VOL. II

# Doug Lennox

THE DUNDURN GROUP
TORONTO

Publisher: Anthony Hawke
Editor: Andrea Pruss
Illustrations: Catriona Wight
Design: Andrew Roberts
Printer: Transcontinental

**Library and Archives Canada Cataloguing in Publication**

Lennox, Doug
  Now you know : the book of answers / Doug Lennox.

ISBN 1-55002-461-2 (v. 1).--ISBN 1-55002-530-9 (v. 2)

  1. Questions and answers.  2. Curiosities and wonders.
I. Title.

AG195.L45 2003        031.02        C2003-903531-X

        3    4    5        08    07    06    05    04

Conseil des Arts du Canada    Canada Council for the Arts    Canadä    ONTARIO ARTS COUNCIL CONSEIL DES ARTS DE L'ONTARIO

We acknowledge the support of the **Canada Council for the Arts** and the **Ontario Arts Council** for our publishing program. We also acknowledge the financial support of the **Government of Canada** through the **Book Publishing Industry Development Program** and **The Association for the Export of Canadian Books,** and the **Government of Ontario** through the **Ontario Book Publishers Tax Credit** program, and the **Ontario Media Development Corporation's Ontario Book Initiative.**

Printed and bound in Canada.⊕
Printed on recycled paper.
www.dundurn.com

Dundurn Press
8 Market Street
Suite 200
Toronto, Ontario, Canada
M5E 1M6

Gazelle Book Services Limited
White Cross Mills
Hightown, Lancaster, England
LA1 4X5

Dundurn Press
2250 Military Road
Tonawanda NY
U.S.A. 14150

This book is dedicated to the memory
of Coralie and Joe Lennox
and to all of my family whose hard lives taught me
that any degree of success or failure is my own responsibility.

"Everything you can imagine will happen to you, but nothing will ever happen the way you imagined."

D.L.

# ACKNOWLEDGEMENTS

I wish to acknowledge the support of Jean-Marie Heimrath, Dawn Schultz, Sheldon Gorlick, and David Steinberg, who cover my back, and to thank the fraternity of radio and television broadcasters who carry the program and who took time to let their audiences know about both these books.

# CONTENTS

# PREFACE

This book is a *second* collection of *new* scripts from the Sound Source Network's popular syndicated radio series "Now You Know," which in book form became a Canadian best-seller.

This second book was encouraged by the response to the first and continues to offer an entertaining and concise insight into the origins of everyday language use, customs, and rituals that traces the subconscious ways we are linked not only to our own ancestors but also to those of all cultures that came before us.

I've always believed that learning is fun, if not essential, and that entertainment can sometimes be nurturing, and so I was overwhelmed by the e-mail and letters from across Canada and around the world, from individuals and major institutes of learning — but never more so than when hearing about an eight-year-old boy who used the first book as a research source for a school project that earned him an A+.

For those of you who bought a copy as a Christmas or birthday gift for you fathers, sons, or husbands, I apologize for having introduced the "Cliff Claven Syndrome" into your homes.

Once again, the scripts that are included within this book have been thoroughly researched but are not academic studies. They are for a quick read and for fun.

If the information in this book entertains you and arouses your curiosity, if you say "I didn't know that," then I have fulfilled my intended purpose because now you will know — *more*.

Doug Lennox 2004

# CUSTOMS

## What is the origin of the engagement ring?

The diamond engagement ring was introduced by the Venetians, who discovered the diamond's value in the sixteenth century, but betrothal gifts hadn't included rings until 860 A.D., when Pope Nicholas I decreed that a ring of value must be given as a statement of nuptial intent and that if the man called off the wedding, the jilted bride kept the ring. If the woman ended the engagement, she was to return the ring and be sent to a nunnery.

## Why does being "turned down" mean rejection?

To be "turned down" comes from an antiquated courting custom followed by our very proper ancestors. When all meetings between young men and women required chaperones, and because aggressive romantic suggestions were forbidden, a man carried a courting mirror, which, at a discreet moment, he would place face up on a table between them. If the woman favoured his advances, the mirror went untouched, but if she had no interest she would turn down the mirror — and the suitor.

## How did throwing confetti become a wedding custom?

Because the main purpose of marriage was to produce children, ancient peoples showered the new bride with fertility symbols such as wheat grain. The Romans baked this wheat into small cakes for the couple, to be eaten in a tradition known as *conferriatio*, or "eating together." The guests then threw handfuls of a mixture of honeyed nuts and dried fruits called *confetto* at the bride, which we copy by throwing confetti.

## Why do brides wear wedding veils?

Although veils for women are today associated with Muslims, their origin goes back at least three thousand years before Mohammed was

even born. Outside of the Middle East, this symbol of modesty had all but disappeared by 400 B.C. when the Romans introduced sheer, translucent veils into the wedding ceremony to remind the woman that she was entering a new life of submission to her husband. Veils predate the wedding dress by several centuries.

## What are the origins of the wedding ring?

A school of thought persists that the first wedding rings were used by barbarians to tether the bride to her captor's home. This may or may not be true, but we do know that around 2800 B.C., because the Egyptians considered a circle to signify eternity, rings were used in marriage ceremonies. The Romans often added a miniature key welded to one side of the bride's ring to signify that she now owned half of her husband's wealth.

### Why do we say that a married couple has "tied the knot"?

In Western culture, "tying the knot" suggests the pledge of inseparable unity made by a married couple. The expression comes from ancient India, when during the wedding ceremony the Hindu groom would put a brightly coloured ribbon around the bride's neck. During the time it took to tie the ribbon into a knot, the bride's father could demand a better price for his daughter, but once the knot was completed the bride became the groom's forever.

### Why, when looking for a showdown, do we say, "I've got a bone to pick"?

Wild pack animals will eat from a carcass only after the alpha male has finished. Having a bone to pick establishes superiority and comes from an ancient Sicilian wedding ritual. At dinner's end, the bride's father would give the groom a bone and instruct him to pick it clean. This ritual signalled the groom's authority over his new wife, establishing that in all future decisions, he would have the final word.

### If most people use a fork in their right hands, why is it set on the left at the table?

When the fork surfaced in the eleventh century, the only eating utensil was a knife, which was used by the right hand to cut and deliver food to the mouth. The left hand was assigned the new fork, which is why it's set on the left. In the mid-nineteenth century, forks finally reached the backwoods of America but without any European rules of etiquette, so settlers used the right hand for both utensils.

### Why do we say "Let's have a ball" when we are looking for a good time?

A "ball" was a medieval religious celebration held on special occasions such as the Feast of Fools at Easter. It was called a ball because the choirboys danced and sang in a ring while catching and returning a ball that was lobbed at them by a church leader (called the ring leader). Although tossing balls during large circular dances became a common folk custom, the only ball at a dance today is the name.

## Why do we cover our mouths and apologize when we yawn?

The yawn is now known to be the body's way of infusing oxygen into a tired body, but suggestion is the only explanation for its contagiousness. To ancient man, who had witnessed many lives leave bodies in a final breath, a yawn signalled that the soul was about to escape through the mouth and death might be prevented by covering it. Because a yawn is contagious, the apology was for passing on the mortal danger to others.

## Why are Christian men required to remove their hats in church?

Removing clothing as an act of subjugation began when the Assyrians routinely humiliated their captives by making them strip naked. The Greeks amended this by requiring their new servants to strip only from the waist up. By the Middle Ages, a serf had to remove only his hat in the presence of his superiors. Following these gestures of respect for the master is the reason Christian men remove their hats in church and why Muslims leave their shoes by the mosque door.

## Why are those who carry the coffin at a funeral called "pallbearers"?

The ancient Sumarians buried their dead in woven baskets that the Greeks called *kophinos*, giving us the word *coffin*. Because people feared that the departed soul was looking to possess a new body, or re-enter his own, the coffin bearers wore hoods and black clothes, then hid the coffin under a black cloth that the Romans called a *pallium*, which gave us the prefix "pall," as in pallbearer.

### Why do people pray with a string of beads?

The *rosary*, or "wreath of roses," first appeared in fifteenth-century Europe, but the practice of reciting prayers with a string of beads or knots goes back about five hundred years before the dawn of Christianity. The word *bead* comes from the Anglo-Saxon word *bidden*, meaning "to ask." The principle for both Christians and Muslims is that the more you ask or repeat a prayer the more effective it is, and so the rosary is an aid in keeping count.

# FOOD & DRINK

**Why is a wiener on a bun called a "hot dog"?**

The evolution of the sausage began in Babylon, and modern incarnations include the Viennese wiener and the frankfurter, which was shaped in the form of a Frankfurt German butcher's pet dachshund. The Dachshund Sausage Dog became very popular in America, where the bun was added in 1904. In 1906, cartoonist Ted Dorgan couldn't spell dachshund, so he simply named his drawing of a dog on a bun covered in mustard a hot dog, and it's been called that ever since.

**Why are drinking glasses sometimes called "tumblers"?**

In 1945, Earl Tupper produced his first polyethylene plastic seven-ounce bathroom tumbler, so called because it could fall or tumble without breaking. But a "tumbler" drinking glass had already been around for centuries before Tupperware. It was specially designed with a round or pointed bottom so that it couldn't stand upright and had to be drunk dry before it could be laid on its side — otherwise it would tumble and spill.

**Is flavour the only reason that lemon is served with fish?**

Although lemon enhances the taste of fish, that isn't the original reason the two were served together. Six hundred years ago, lemon was introduced with fish as a safety precaution. People believed that if someone swallowed a bone, a mouthful of lemon juice would dissolve it. We now know that this isn't the case, but we also understand why they believed it. Sucking on a lemon causes the throat muscles to contort, helping to dislodge any stuck bone.

**Why is alcohol called "spirits" and empty beer bottles "dead soldiers"?**

After a bachelor party there are a lot of "dead soldiers," or empty beer bottles, lying around. They are dead because the alcohol, or spirit, has left their bodies. The spirit, like the soul, was considered the independent and invisible essence of everything physical and is quite separate from the material fact. A beer bottle without its alcohol has lost its spirit and, just like any other creation human or otherwise, has dearly departed.

### Why is enhancing a food's taste called "seasoning"?

When the Gauls found that some food tastes could be improved through aging or the passing of the seasons, they called it *saisonner*. After being conquered by the Normans in 1066, the British called the new aging process "seasoning." With the introduction of Middle Eastern spices from returning Crusaders in the thirteenth century, seasoning took on the meaning of anything that embellishes the taste of food.

## Where are the breeding waters of the species of fish known as "sardines"?

The name "sardines" is used in reference to over twenty species of fish, and so they breed everywhere. A can of sardines is filled with one of dozens of species of immature ocean fish that happen to get caught in a trawler's net, including pilchard and herring. The same is true of freshwater smelts, which are scooped up by the thousands along inland waterways after hatching in the spring and then fried as a delicacy in butter.

## Why do we describe warm food as "piping hot"?

Today, piping hot usually means comfortably warm food straight from your own oven to the table, but it took a few centuries to evolve into that meaning. There was a time when everyone bought freshly baked bread every day from a neighbourhood or village baker. When the bread was ready, the baker would signal from his front door by blowing on a pipe or horn, which caused people to hurry to get bread before it ran out and gave us the expression "piping hot."

## Does Canadian beer taste better than American beer because it has more alcohol?

Canadian beer might feel better than American beer, but its fuller taste comes from its ingredients. Canadian beer is brewed with 50 percent more malt barley than its watery American cousin, which relies more on corn. Regular Canadian beer has an alcohol-by-volume content of 5 percent, while American beer is 4.5 percent. A standard European beer is fuller still, with a 5.2 percent alcohol content. Canadian light beer is 4 percent, while American light is 3.8 percent.

### Why is a pint of American beer smaller than one that's Canadian?

Since the adoption of the metric system, pints have become rare in Canada. Liquids are usually measured in litres, but the American pint is smaller than the one in Canada because in 1824, when the British introduced the imperial gallon to the world (including Canada), American pride refused to go along with the change. Instead, they kept the outdated original and smaller English gallon from colonial times.

### Why do we say, "That takes the cake" when something's done exceptionally well?

African Americans of the Old South highlighted their social season with a dancing contest called a cakewalk. The contestants often practised for months and included couples of all ages. The prize was a huge cake which was set in the centre of the hall and around which the dancers exhibited their skills. A panel of judges would watch the innovative dancers until a winner was chosen, who would then "take the cake."

### Why do we say that something special is "the apple of your eye"?

For centuries it was believed that the pupil of the eye was solid and spherical like an apple, so that's what they called it. Therefore, anything or anyone compared to it would indeed be very special. In the Bible, the expression is part of a song spoken by Moses: "He found him in a desert land, and in the howling waste of the wilderness; he encircled him, he cared for him, and kept him as the apple of His eye."

### Why when humiliated are we forced to "eat humble pie"?

"Humble pie" is an Americanization of the original English expression "umble pie," a staple in the diet of very poor people during the eleventh century. After bringing down a deer, only the men could eat the choice meat from the kill; women and children were fed the innards, or the umbles, which they seasoned and baked into a pie. To be forced to eat umble pie was to be placed among the lowest in the social order.

## Why do the Chinese use chopsticks instead of cutlery?

While Europeans were still cutting up carcasses on the dinner table, the Chinese had for centuries considered the practice barbaric. A Chinese proverb, "We sit at the dinner table to eat, not cut up carcasses," dictated that eating should be simplified, and so food was cut into bite sizes in the kitchen before serving. The chopstick (from *kwai-tsze*, which means "quick ones") was the perfect instrument to convey this pre-cut food to the mouth.

## Why are potatoes called both "spuds" and "taters"?

Back in the fifteenth century a *spud* was a short-handled spade that had a general use but was best known for digging up potatoes. People who sold potatoes were called spuddies. In Britain, *taters* means cold, and — as is suggested in the rhyme "potatoes in the mould equals cold" — potatoes when grown in the mould, which is topsoil, are colder than if they'd grown deeper in the ground; therefore, cold spuds are taters.

## Why is cornbread sometimes called "Johnny cake"?

Cornbread, or "Johnny cake," is a country comfort food that was given to the first North American settlers by the Natives. The cake was and is made principally of maize or corn and was baked on a heated flat stone from an open fire. The white trappers who first tasted cornbread were guests of the Shawnee tribe and so they called it Shawnee cake, which soon became a staple with the settlers as the mispronounced Johnny cake.

## Why is a large cup called a "mug"?

A mug is a large drinking cup with a handle and is most commonly used to drink coffee, although it's not unknown to beer drinkers. "A mug" is also slang for the face. In the eighteenth century, drinking vessels were shaped and painted to look like the heads of pirates or local drunks or even despised public officials or politicians. Now called "Toby jugs," these cups with faces became known simply as mugs.

# PEOPLE & PLACES

**Why is the city of Toronto called "Hogtown" with an area known as "Cabbagetown"?**

Toronto became "Hogtown" in the 1890s, when meat packing was one of the city's principal industries. Animals of all kinds, including the squealing hogs, were off-loaded at the railway yard to be processed and shipped back out as hams. The central, upper-class, urban area known as "Cabbagetown" took its name from the gardens of the poor Irish immigrants who settled there and grew potatoes and cabbages to survive.

**What do a "one-horse" and a "jerkwater" town have in common?**

In the early days of the railroad, huge tanks were built along the routes where the steam engines could stop and refill by pulling, or jerking, a spout into place, allowing the water to flow from the tank to the engine. The tiny community that grew up around the tank was called a "jerkwater" town. A "one-horse" town was so small, one horse could do all the work and transportation for the entire community, so it was about the size of a jerkwater town.

**What is the difference between "uptown" and "downtown"?**

When New York City was only a town, its growth was restricted by the shape of Manhattan Island. The word *uptown* first appeared in about 1830 and was used to describe the residential area growing up the Island away from the southern business centre. Within a few years, *downtown* appeared to describe the opposite of uptown, or the main commercial district. Today, the suburbs are uptown, while downtown remains the heart of the business district.

## Why is a sleazy area of town known as the "red-light district"?

In the early days of the railroad, steam trains made quick stops in small towns for water or to pick up passengers and cargo. The crew would use this time to dash to the saloon or to make a quick visit to the local brothel. While doing their business, the trainmen would hang their lit red kerosene lanterns outside so that the train would-n't leave without them, and this is how areas practising prostitution became known as red-light districts.

## Why are natives of Nova Scotia called "Bluenosers"?

The famous schooner on the Canadian dime took its name from the natives of the province of Nova Scotia, who are called Bluenosers. The reason for this is that at one time, the province's chief export was a type of potato that featured a protruding blue end, which resembled a nose. As for the proud schooner *Bluenose*, she earned her way onto the dime by outracing the American schooner *Elsie* to become the fastest fishing boat on earth.

## Why is someone we consider slow called a "dunce"?

A *dunce* still means someone we consider out of step, and it derives unfairly from Duns Scotus, the name of a brilliant thirteenth-century Scottish philosopher who, along with his followers (who were called "Duns men"), resisted the thinking within the Renaissance that swept the Middle Ages. In a practice as unfair as the sight of a child in a conical dunce cap, Scotus was ridiculed for being different and for daring to express his own thoughts.

## Why are aristocrats of the ruling classes called "bluebloods"?

The name *bluebloods* refers to the pallor of the Spanish ruling classes after the conquest of the darker skinned Moors. After the blood in them loses oxygen while flowing back to the heart, the veins of fair or untanned people whose skin is never exposed to the sun appear blue, while the veins of those with darker complexions, like the Moors, are less obvious. Their blue blood distinguished true Spanish aristocracy from the conquering Moors.

## Why is someone with a drinking problem called a "lush"?

In eighteenth-century London there was an actors' drinking club called The City of Lushington, which may have taken its name from Dr. Thomas Lushington, a prominent drinker from the seventeenth century whose descendants became brewers of fine ale. *Lush*, the abbreviation of *Lushington*, became a common slang reference for beer in early England. It later crossed the ocean, where in America the term *lush* became a reference to a heavy drinker.

## Why is an institution of learning called a "kindergarten" or a "school" and referred to by students as their "alma mater"?

It all starts in *kindergarten*, a German concept meaning "children's garden," where the atmosphere for learning should be as pleasant for a child as being in a garden. *School* follows the same philosophy and is from a Greek word for leisure. When university students refer to their *alma maters*, they are speaking Latin for "nursing mother," in this case one which nourishes the mind.

## Why are some university graduates and most unmarried men called "bachelors"?

In the eleventh century, a bachelor was a low-ranking knight without the means to raise an army. To indicate this he flew a pointed banner, whereas a full knight had a flag without a tip. The bachelor was a junior, which is why a bachelor's degree refers to the lowest rank from a university. Because most young men were unmarried, they began being referred to as bachelors in the fourteenth century.

### Why is a religious woman who lives in a convent and vows poverty, chastity, and obedience called a "nun"?

Women who are sisters within a strict religious order today are called nuns, a word that has evolved through time to mean compassion and kindness. In Sanskrit, *nana* meant "mother," and it is often still used today as an endearment for grandmothers. In Latin, *nonna* means "child's nurse," again still used in the form *nanny*. In Greek, *nane* simply meant "good." All of these gave us the word *nun* to describe the strength and good intentions of the religious vocation.

### Why do we call someone who sells illegal alcohol a "bootlegger"?

During the prohibition period of the 1920s, those who sold illegal booze became very wealthy, but the term *bootlegger* came out of the nineteenth century, when it was the fashion for horsemen to wear very high boots. These boots were commonly used to conceal pints of illegal bottled moonshine by both the purveyor and the customer and gave us the term *bootleg*, which now means anything sold outside the law.

### Why is a bootleg joint called a "blind pig"?

In 1838, Massachusetts outlawed the sale of hard liquor, causing drinkers to find creative ways to buy and sell booze. One entrepreneur set up a booth with a sign offering, for a small fee, a glimpse of an amazing striped pig. Those who paid to enter found a glass of rum standing next to a painted clay pig. The pig saw nothing, so the transaction was safe, and the expression "blind pig" was born.

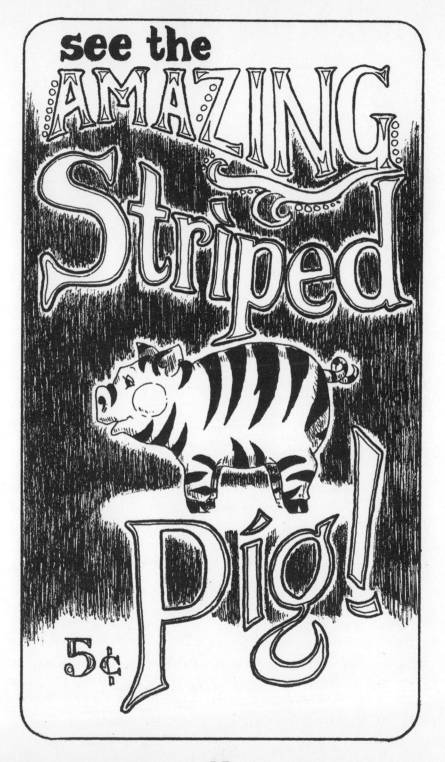

### Why is a worthless bully called a "thug"?

In India, the British encountered a sinister sect that worshipped the Hindu goddess of death. Known as *thags* in Hindi, they robbed their victims then strangled them with a silk scarf. Indian authorities wouldn't suppress them, and so in the 1830s, the British wiped them out by hanging four hundred and imprisoning thousands. The American press picked up the story, and *thags* became *thugs*, a generic term for "hoods."

### Why are men and boys called "guys"?

Every November 5, the British celebrate the 1605 foiling of a plot to blow up the parliament buildings by Guy Fawkes. As part of the festivities, an effigy of Fawkes dressed in rags and old mismatched clothes was paraded through the streets and then burned on a bonfire. By 1830, any man who was badly dressed was being referred to as a "guy," meaning he looked as disheveled as the effigy of Guy Fawkes.

### Why is a pretentious person called a "snob"?

A snob is someone who pretends wealth and demands respect he doesn't deserve. Universities only educated children of the nobility until Cambridge opened its doors to commoners in the seventeenth century. These new students were required to register in Latin as *Sine Nobilitate*, which means "without nobility." Abbreviated, this Latin phrase is *S.Nob*, pronounced "snob," and it took on the meaning of anyone above his station.

### Why are the stalwart defenders of a status quo referred to as "the Old Guard"?

"The Old Guard" suggests an outdated group defending something whose time has passed, but the expression began in glory at the battle of Waterloo. Known for their fierce loyalty to Napoleon, the Imperial Guard was composed of the Young Guard, the Middle Guard, and the Old Guard. It was the Old Guard from this group who mounted the final brave but hopeless French charge at the Battle of Waterloo.

## Why are weather forecasters called "meteorologists"?

Meteorology became the science of forecasting weather during the fourth century B.C., when it was believed that dramatic heavenly events were the cause of everything, especially weather — and there was nothing more dramatic than the arrival of a meteor. In Greek, *meteorology* means "a discourse from high in the air." Studying meteors to predict weather ended in the late seventeenth century, but weather forecasters are still known as meteorologists.

## Why are frenzied women referred to as "hysterical" but not equally frenetic men?

The physicians of ancient Greece considered hysteria to be an exclusively female problem caused by a disorder within the woman's distinctive internal organs. *Hystera* is the Greek word for womb and survives today in the medical procedure *hysterectomy*. Men suffer the antisocial symptoms of hysteria less frequently than women, but when they do, they are called sociopaths.

## Why is a small child called a "little shaver"?

During the period when settlers spent a lot of time cutting wood, if a son looked or acted like his father he was called a "chip off the old block," meaning that except for size, the two were as clearly related as a chip cut from its original block of wood from the family tree. A little shaver is the same, except that a shaving is smaller than a chip. A "sprig," on the other hand, is a child too small yet to even have a branch on the family tree.

### Why is an unidentified person referred to as "John Doe"?

"John Doe" is the name used to describe someone within legal circumstances when the true name is either unknown or indiscreet to reveal. The practice dates back to British courts in the early nineteenth century, when John and Jane Doe were used as names for unknown or unclear defendants in real estate eviction disputes. "Doe" was an extremely rare name, and there is nothing to suggest that any real John Doe ever existed.

### Why are prison informers referred to as "finks"?

A *fink*, whether in prison or not, is a derogatory reference to someone who seeks favour from the authorities for information that they have learned in confidence. It's said that a fink is someone who sings to the police or the boss like a canary, which all becomes logical when you realize that *fink* is the Yiddish word for "finch." Finches, or finks, are a family of songbirds, of which the canary is one of the most vocal.

### Why were women warriors called "Amazons"?

Homer created the ancient Greek myth of fierce women warriors known as Amazons. *Amazon* is made up from A, meaning "without," and *mazos*, meaning "breast," because legend has it that they removed one breast to better throw a spear or use a bow and arrow. Amazons only visited men to become pregnant, and at birth only girl children were allowed to live to be raised by the Amazon warriors' mothers.

### Why is the presiding officer of a committee called a "chairman"?

Whether it's a chairman or a chairwoman, that person is in the seat of authority and has been since the fourteenth century. At that time a *chair* was a throne (it came from the Greek word *kathedra*, leading to the word *cathedral* for the place housing the seat of the bishop). In business, the person in charge sat in a comfortable armed chair, while everyone else sat on stools, and so he took the esteemed title "chairman."

## Why is a person who takes punishment for someone else called a "fall guy"?

Since the 1880s, "taking a fall" has meant to be arrested or imprisoned. To take a fall now figuratively means to be taken down for something you may or may not have done, but a fall guy, like a professional wrestler, has been paid or framed to take punishment. On a movie set, a fall guy is a stuntman who again is paid to literally take the fall, sometimes from high buildings, for another actor.

## Why were young women from the Roaring Twenties called "flappers"?

The 1920s was a breakout decade for young women who'd just won the right to vote. The era evokes images of young flappers like the cartoon character Betty Boop, who was only sixteen, wildly dancing to the Charleston. They were called flappers because of the way they resembled a baby duck flapping its wings before being able to fly. *Flapper* is a very old word meaning a girl too young to conceive.

## Why are only citizens of the United States called "Americans"?

After discarding dozens of suggestions, Canada took its name from the Native American word *kanata*. The most popular of the names considered by the United States was Columbia, which is why the nation's capital is located in the District of Columbia. But because they couldn't make a final decision, the people of the United States have accepted the unofficial name given to them by the British during the war of independence. They are, simply, Americans.

## What is the difference between a "bum," a "tramp," and a "hobo"?

During the Great Depression of the 1930s, Godfrey Irwin published *American Tramp and Underworld Slang*, within which he explained the difference. Bums loaf and sit; tramps loaf and walk; but a hobo moves and works. *Hobo* is derived from *hoeboy*, because many of the young men travelling the rails were from farms and carried a hoe with them so that they could work the gardens of those households that might employ them.

## Why is a spineless coward called a "wimp"?

Someone who is weak and indecisive is often called a wimp, which is a short form of the word *whimpering*. The origin of *wimp* is a series of children's books written in the 1890s by Evelyn Sharp, which featured characters called Wymps who loved playing practical jokes on others but who would cry when jokes were played on them. In the 1930s, a corpulent Popeye cartoon character named J. Wellington "Wimpy" kept the word alive.

## Why is a small-time player called a "piker"?

Many early highways had entrances that were blocked by a pike, or long pole, which was "turned," or opened, after a toll was paid. These highways were called turnpikes. Those who walked these roads were sometimes vagrants and very often unsophisticated farm boys on their way to seek their fortunes in the city. If you just "came down the pike" you were naive and often admonished as a "piker."

### Why is a work supervisor called a "straw boss"?

A straw boss is usually a supervisor or foreman of menial work, and the label comes from the farm. The "big boss" was in charge of the entire threshing crew, whose main task was to harvest the wheat from the chaff, which was straw. The "straw boss" was in charge of the secondary crew, whose job it was to gather and bail the discarded by-product. "Straw boss" has come to mean a petty supervisor without any real authority.

### Why are the names of those out of favour said to be kept in a "black book" or on a "blacklist"?

The "blacklisting" of artists by the American Congress during the 1950s was a shameful and well documented reign of terror, but black-lists and little black books are still quietly with us, especially among those who see enemies everywhere. It began with King Henry VIII of England, whose infamous black book recorded so-called abuses in monasteries to justify his purge against the Catholic Church.

### Why is a speaker's platform known as a "rostrum"?

After a victory at sea the Romans customarily removed the decorative prow or *rostrum* from defeated enemy ships to be returned to Rome as symbols of their supremacy on the high seas. These *rostra* were displayed on the speaker's platform in the Roman Forum until there were so many that the stage from which a speaker addressed the assembly became known as the rostrum, or the ship's prow.

### What is the difference between a "ghost writer" and a "hack writer"?

A ghost writer is a craftsman who writes speeches or books for another person who gets the credit as author. Although well paid, they're called "ghosts" because they're invisible. In the fourteenth century, while there were warhorses and draft or workhorses, an ordinary rented riding horse was known as a "hackney" or a "hack." The word *hack* came to mean anything for hire, including writers who did commercial work of any kind to support their efforts at art.

POP CULTURE

## How did Hollywood get its name?

"Hollywood" is a synonym for fantasy for some and decadence for others, yet the dream capital acquired its name from strangers on a train and became a gesture of love between a husband and a wife. In 1887, Mrs. Harvey Wilcox, whose husband owned the California land, overheard the woman next to her on a train refer to her summer home as "Hollywood." Mrs. Wilcox liked the name Hollywood so much that her husband gave it to their California property.

## In movie credits, what are the actual jobs of the gaffer, the key grip, and the best boy?

Filmmaking requires precision teamwork, and each credit is well earned. In movie language, a *gaffer* is the chief electrician; it evolved from the German word *granfer*, meaning "grandfather." A *grip* requires strength, because he or she builds and dismantles scenery and handles other physical chores that require a strong grip. A *best boy* is the gaffer's or grip's assistant.

## How did *dude* become a greeting between buddies?

The word *dude* originated as a Victorian slang word for a man who was effeminate. It's a variation of *dud* or *duds*, from the Arabic word for cloak (*dudde*), and was a reference to fancy or foppish clothes. When vain, fashion-conscious city slickers wanted a taste of the West, they went to a Dude Ranch. *Dude* was kept alive by California surfers and took on its current fellowship meaning from a generation weaned on the *Teenage Mutant Ninja Turtles*.

## Who was Pansy O'Hara in *Gone With The Wind*?

Margaret Mitchell was a first-time writer when in 1936 she submitted a manuscript of Civil War stories told to her by her grandfather under the title *Tomorrow Is Another Day*, featuring a Southern belle named Pansy O'Hara. The publisher convinced her to change the book's name to *Gone With The Wind*, a line from a nineteenth-century poem by Ernest Dowson, and, after a bitter argument, to change "Pansy" to "Scarlett."

**Who were detective Sherrinford Holmes and Ormand Sacker?**

When Arthur Conan Doyle began writing mystery novels, he chose one of his medical school instructors, Dr. Joseph Bell, as his sleuth's model and named him Sherrinford Holmes. His assistant, Watson, took his name from one of Bell's assistants, but not before being briefly named Ormand Sacker. Incidentally, in none of the stories does Holmes ever say, "Elementary, my dear Watson." That was used only in the movies.

## What were the origins of vaudeville?

Tony Pastor introduced vaudeville in New York in 1861. The word *vaudeville* is an Americanization of *Vau de Vire*, the valley of the Vau River in Normandy, which became famous in the fifteenth century for the comedic songs of Olivier Basselin. An 1883 vaudeville bill from Boston's Gaiety Museum featured a midget named Baby Alice, a stuffed mermaid, two comedians, and a chicken with a human face. From these humble beginnings would emerge the great American theatre.

## Why is Batman's hometown called Gotham City?

"Gotham City" is a nickname for New York and was introduced by Washington Irving in 1807 as the home of fast-talking know-it-alls. Irving took the name from a legend about King John, who wanted to build a regal estate near the actual Gotham in England but was discouraged when the citizens, not wanting to pay the added taxes, enacted a plan of feigning madness (like real New Yorkers), which caused the king to change his mind in a "Gotham minute."

## Why is a citrus soft drink called 7-Up?

In 1929, Charles L. Grigg of St Louis began selling a lemon-lime soft drink under the slogan "Takes the Ouch out of Grouch," and it became a sensation. One of the soft drink's key ingredients was lithium, a powerful anti-depressant, which was removed in the 1940s. The "7" in the name means seven ounces, while the "Up" is a reference to the carbonated bubbles rising to the surface.

## What was the original meaning of "rock and roll"?

American slaves communicated secret codes past their white masters with music, and in 1951, when Alan Freed coined the phrase "rock and roll," he was doing the same thing. In blues and jazz, the words mean "having great sex" (*Good Rockin' Tonight*, 1948, and *My Man Rocks Me With One Steady Roll*, 1922). These coded lyrics were unfamiliar to the white broadcasters and gave Freed a way to cross the colour barrier and introduce white kids to rhythm and blues, where they soon learned how to *Rock Around The Clock*.

### How did the Barbie doll get its name?

Barbie was designed by Ruth Handler and named after her daughter. However, she didn't realize that the original moulds came from an existing German doll named Lili, a popular cartoon prostitute of the time. At first stores refused to stock the anatomically correct doll, until it was neutralized in 1959. By the way, Barbie's measurements if she were life-sized are 39-23-33 ... still pretty sexy.

### Why did Charles Schulz name his Charlie Brown comic strip *Peanuts*?

Charlie Brown first appeared as a character in a syndicated cartoon in September of 1950, which was named *Li'l Folks*. The most popular children's television show at the time was *Howdy Doody*, and the syndicator insisted that the strip be renamed for the kids in Doody's cordoned-off area for his live children's audience, which was called the "peanut gallery." And so the most popular comic strip in history became known as *Peanuts*.

### What is the origin of the name of the popular ice cream Haagen-Daazs?

In the 1960s, Reuben Mattas, a Polish-born American from the Bronx, was struggling to sell his quality ice cream when he took note of the popularity of all things Danish modern. He decided to tap into the fad by putting a map of Denmark on his cartons and calling it Haagen-Daazs. Of course, there's no such Danish word as Haagen-Daazs, but this inspiration of marketing genius became a billion-dollar idea.

## How did the Singing Chipmunks get their names, and who are the namesakes of Rocky and Bullwinkle?

The Singing Chipmunks were inspired by a near accident when their creator, Ross Bagdasarian, had to swerve sharply to miss hitting a chipmunk while driving on a country road. He named the trio Alvin, Simon, and Theodore after three record company executives. As for Rocky and Bullwinkle, their creator, Jay Ward, named them after fighter Rocky Graziano and used car salesman Clarence Bullwinkle.

## Why are shopping centres called "malls"?

Shopping centres mushroomed in the 1950s but weren't called malls until 1967. *Mall* comes from the popular sixteenth-century Italian ball and mallet game *palamaglio*, which came to England as *pall-mall* (pronounced "pell mell"). By the eighteenth century the game had been forgotten, except on the name of a London street where it had been played and on a parallel ritzy avenue named the Mall, where fashionable aristocrats strolled and shopped.

## Why is something pleasing said to be "cool"?

*Cool*, like *groovy*, was a very popular expression of satisfaction during the 1960s and early '70s, but only the former lives on. *Cool* surfaced in the early nineteenth century and, like *groovy*, which meant "in the groove," as in a smoothly played vinyl record, it was popularized in the modern era by bebop jazz musicians in the 1940s. Cool means unfazed and under control, like being on ice, which is real cool.

## What is the origin of the word *jazz*?

Jazz may be an American art form, but the word predates any application to music or sex. It first appeared in print in 1831 as *jazzing*, meaning the telling of fun stories. The first American use of *jazz* was in baseball as slang for enthusiasm in 1913. Its first musical use was a year later, to describe the vigor of West Coast band leader Art Hickman. The word *jazz* wasn't used to describe black music until 1918.

## What are the origins of the Tony and the Emmy awards?

The Tony Awards are named in honor of the prominent Broadway personality Antoinette Perry, whose nickname was Tony. The Tony Awards began in 1947, the year after her death. When the Emmy Awards were introduced in the 1940s they were called Immies, after the word *image* in "Image Orthocon Tube," an important part of a television camera. Over time the Immy became an Emmy.

## Where did the yellow smiley face come from?

The yellow smiley face, with its dotted black eyes, first appeared with a slightly crooked smile as a promotion for the deejays of radio station WMCA in New York in 1962. However, in 1963, commercial artist Harvey Ball introduced the version that's still with us when he curved the smile as a promotion for a major insurance company. Unable to copyright his smiley face, Ball received forty-five dollars for its creation.

## Why does Tonto call the Lone Ranger "Kemo Sabe"?

In 1933, during the Great Depression, radio station WXYZ in Detroit introduced *The Lone Ranger*. His faithful Native companion, Tonto, was supposed to have been from the Potawatomi tribe, but linguistic scholars were stumped by his reference to the Lone Ranger as *Kemo Sabe*. Co-creator Jim Jewell eventually confessed that he had made up the expression from the name of his father-in-law's summer camp, Ke-Mo-Sah-Bee.

## Why is hair trimmed straight across the forehead called "bangs"?

Since the beginning of the nineteenth century, a *bobtail* has described a horse with a tail cut very short, while a long but neatly trimmed tail has been called a *bangtail*. The "bang" refers to the quickness of the cut. The Americans abbreviated bangtail to *bangs* in 1878 when hair cut straight across the human forehead became popular. Like the ponytail, bangs is a hairstyle borrowed from the business end of a horse.

## Why is the energy from a car's engine referred to as "horse-power"?

When Scottish inventor James Watt received a patent on his steam engine in 1755, horses were being used to draw coal to a mine's surface. After calculating that one horse had the power to haul 330 pounds 100 feet in one minute, he proved that one steam engine could replace an entire herd of horses. This made Watt wealthy and gave us a formula to interpret engine capacity in horsepower.

# ENTERTAINMENT & LEISURE

## Why are skilled computer fanatics called "geeks"?

Since the fifteenth century, *geek* or *geck* has described a low-life fool. For example, a geek is, in carnival slang, someone who bites off the heads of chickens or snakes. At the beginning of the computer age, the word *geek* took on the meaning of a socially awkward intellectual. But through accepting and celebrating their geek status, skilled computer operators have managed to change the meaning of the word, so that a geek is someone to be admired.

## Why do we call leisure work a "hobby"?

*Hobby* is a word used to describe an avocation done for diversion or self-pleasure. Few people find fulfillment working for someone else, and so many express their individuality within a hobby. The word comes from a toy made from a stick with a horse's head that children used to ride. It was called a hobby horse, and, like the child at play, anyone pursuing a hobby was doing it for escapism and pleasure, not money.

## Why is a commercial record player called a "jukebox"?

Jukeboxes first appeared in restaurants and bars in the late 1930s. *Juke* is an African word meaning "to make wicked mischief" and came directly from American slaves, who described the illegal brothels or bootlegger shacks where they could occasionally escape their cruel lives with a jar of moonshine as "Juke-joints." *Juke* had an exotic and forbidden appeal, which inspired the name jukebox.

## Why is the word *trump* used in card games, and what else in the deck, other than the cards, adds up to fifty-two?

A trump card or suit has been designated a higher rank than usual for the purposes of the game being played and will triumph over others of normally equal value. *Trump* is a distortion of the word *triumph*. If you add up the number of letters in the names of the cards, the total is fifty-two, the same as the number of cards in the deck (acetwothreefour-fivesixseveneightninetenjackqueenking).

## Why is a particular game of gambling with cards called "poker"?

A card game called poque was introduced to America by French gamblers in New Orleans. Both the name and the game came from the German word *pochspiel*, which literally means "boast game," while the derivative *pochen* means "to knock." This knock on the table is still part of the many forms of poker and indicates that a player is passing on a bet. In a Southern drawl, poque was "pok-uh," which, when spread to the rest of the country, became "poker."

## Why do we say that a poker player, or anyone putting up a false front, is "bluffing"?

The word *bluff* is from the Dutch word *bluffen*, meaning to deceive, and entered English as a nautical reference to the imposing front of a warship. For the same reason, the term *bluff* was applied to a bold coastline that rose straight and high out of the water. By the 1830s, bluffing had taken on the meaning of anything less intimidating than it appears and had entered the game of poker as a reference to the art of deception.

## Why is a shifty person called a "four flusher"?

In poker, five cards from the same suit is called a flush and is very valuable. The highest possible poker hand is a royal flush, or five cards from ten to ace all from the same suit. However, four cards from the same suit, or a four flush, is nearly worthless. If a person continues to play with such a hand they are bluffing, or hiding the truth, which gave us the expression "four flusher" for someone not to be trusted or believed.

## Why are cigars called "stogies"?

Tobacco was picked up from the natives of the East Indies and introduced to Europe by the Spanish in the sixteenth century. The English word *cigar* is from the Spanish *cigarro*, which they took from *cigarrales*, a Cuban word meaning a place of leisure. *Stogie* is an abbreviation of Conestoga, and because the drivers of that wagon company (based in tobacco country) always had a roll-your-own cigar stuck in their mouths, observers called them stogies.

## Why is a tough, all-terrain vehicle called a "Jeep"?

In 1937, the Army introduced a general purpose four-wheel drive vehicle which, when abbreviated, became G.P. At the same time the very popular *Popeye* cartoon had introduced Eugene the Jeep as a weird little pet for Olive Oil; it communicated by calling "jeep." The young men in the service put the little G.P. and the cartoon character together and called the vehicle a Jeep.

## What is the origin of the Frisbee?

In 1870, Frisbee's New England bakery sold pies in round tins, which students at nearby Yale took to tossing as a pastime. In the 1940s, the Wham-O toy company was trying to capitalize on the new UFO mania by selling a plastic flying saucer. When Wham-O noticed Yale students tossing the metal pie plates, they trademarked the name Frisbee and mass-produced the discs in plastic — and a craze was born.

## How did "betting your shirt" come mean to gambling everything you own?

In 1823, the bitterness that led to the Civil War surfaced during a match race between the Northern horse American Eclipse and a Southern colt named Sir Henry. The grudge match inspired fortunes to be wagered, including that of congressman John Randolph, who put up $10,000 and his entire wardrobe, which gave a newspaper the observation that he was "betting his shirt" on the race. (Incidentally, the race was won by American Eclipse, and Randolph kept his wardrobe.)

## Why is a theatre ticket booth called a "box office"?

In early Elizabethan times, theatres admitted the general public into the ground level "pit" without charge. Before the play began, a plate was passed through the mostly standing pit audience and, like a church collection, an established amount was expected for different seats and rows. For the wealthy patrons who bought private balcony boxes for the season, tickets were conveniently held near the entrance in what was called the box office.

## Why do we call a working vacation a "busman's holiday"?

*Bus* is an abbreviation of *omnibus*, which is what they called the original horse-drawn vehicles used for public transportation. The busman, of course, was the driver, and because the bus was drawn by the driver's own horses, he was very concerned about their well-being. It wasn't uncommon for busmen to frequently come down to the barn during their vacation time to ensure that their horses were being well treated, which gave us the expression "busman's holiday."

## Why do actors say "break a leg" when wishing each other good luck?

"Break a leg" comes from the First World War, when, before flying, German airmen wished each other a "broken neck and a broken leg." Considering the dangers of combat with primitive aircraft, this was preferable to losing your life, which was all too common. After the war, the phrase was picked up by actors in the German theatre and eventually adopted by the British and American stages, where it was abbreviated to "break a leg."

## How is "the full monty" related to "three-card monte"?

"The full monty," popularized as a movie title, is a British expression meaning "the whole thing." It came from illegal gambling, where the huge pot of a high stakes game was called the *monty*, from the Spanish word for mountain, which is *monte*. To win the monty meant you had won a mountain of money. Three-card monte, an illegal con game, has the same Spanish origin and refers to the same thing.

## How did the letters in Scrabble get assigned their quantities and numerical values?

In 1931, an unemployed American architect named Alfred Butts invented the game we now call Scrabble. Turned down by every manufacturer he approached, he sold homemade sets out of his garage until 1946, when a company bought the rights and began mass production. Butts determined the scoring value and quantity of each letter by counting the number of times it was used on a single page of the *New York Times*.

**What was the original purpose of Rubik's Cube?**

In 1980, Rubik's Cube became a worldwide craze. Its Hungarian inventor, Professor Erno Rubick, had created the cube as a math aid for his students. After realizing the cube's potential as a toy, he sold two million in Hungary alone before introducing it to the West, making him the Communist world's first self-made millionaire. The Rubik's Cube has over forty-three quintillion configurations (43,252,003,274,489,856,000).

**Why is a superficial vacation known as a "Cook's tour"?**

When Thomas Cook founded the world's first travel agency in 1841 he organized a railway trip for a group of non-drinkers into the British midlands. Soon the safety and security of travelling in groups encouraged the less adventurous to see the world. The more seasoned travellers, enamoured of their ideas of individual adventure, scoffed at these disciplined tours and referred to them sarcastically as "Cook's tours."

# SPORTS

**Why are both the manager of an athletic team and a large passenger vehicle called a "coach"?**

The word *coach* comes from the Hungarian village of Kocs (pronounced "kotch"), made famous for its large, horse-drawn carriages in the sixteenth century. In Britain, the word became *coach*, and by the nineteenth century took on the second meaning of a sports trainer or private tutor. The implication is that, through his experience and knowledge, the coach, like a bus or a train car, carries the younger trainees to their destinations.

**Why are the victors in a competition called "champions"?**

A boxing champion is, of course, the best in his class, but the word has a more honourable history than its use in sports. Derived from the Latin word *campus*, which refers to an open field where battles were fought, the word *champion* passed into French before being adopted into English in the thirteenth century. Its meaning was "one who fights on behalf of another" or "one who defends a person or a cause."

**Why do we say that someone well conditioned has been "whipped into shape"?**

During the ancient Olympics, athletes were expected to go into training ten months before the start of the games. The last month was spent at the site, where — regardless of the weather or bodily injuries, while on a strictly limited diet, and without shoes, shorts, or the right to complain — whenever they faltered, they were whipped by their trainers. These Olympians were literally whipped into shape.

**What is the origin of the sporting term "round robin"?**

A round robin tournament is one in which everyone is treated equally. Each player must face every other player. This democratic process originated in the British Navy in the sixteenth century as a way of petitioning against grievances without being charged with mutiny. The names on the petition were all signed in a circle so that the captain couldn't tell who was the first to sign and thus who initiated the complaint. The sailors named this document a round robin.

### Why is the outcome of a game known as the "score"?

Scores are tallied to decide the winner of a game. *Tally* is from *talea*, the Latin word for stick. *Scoring* is the act of cutting notches or nicks onto that stick to keep track. A stick was sometimes split down the middle so a creditor and debtor could keep an honest tally by notching transactions at the same time. In sport, the side with the most scores or notches cut into a tally stick was the winner.

### Where do the golf terms "par" and "bogey" come from?

Until the introduction of the modern golf ball in 1898, an average score for any given hole was called a *bogey*, the Scottish word for ghost, meaning that the challenge was within the individual player against an unseen opponent. The modern ball took one less stroke to reach the hole, so the new standard was called *par*, a short form of *parity*, meaning equal. Bogey was kept as meaning the original average with the old cloth-covered ball, or one shot over the new ball average of par.

### How is par determined for each hole on a golf course?

Par is the number of strokes a good golfer should make on a particular hole, and it's based on distance. A par 3 hole is up to 250 yards for men and 210 yards for women. A par 4 is 250 to 470 yards for men and between 210 and 400 yards for women. Par 5 is for holes over 470 yards for men and over 400 for women.

### Why do golf balls have dimples?

Original golf balls were made of wood, and it wasn't until the nineteenth century that they evolved through a number of changes. They went from wet feathers stuffed into wet leather for shrinking to "gutties," balls made from a Malaysian form of rubber. At this point someone noticed that the new ball flew further when scuffed up after being hit a few times, and so dimples were added to encourage distance by imitating a well-used ball.

### Why does a golf "duffer" need a "handicap"?

The word *duffer* was once used to describe a counterfeit coin and was expanded to include a worthless person, who, like the counterfeit coin, was only taking up space — such as a duffer on a golf course. Because they are inferior, duffers need a *handicap*, or help, which is really a penalty against the superior players. The word *handicap* came from drawing of lots for positions in a horserace, which literally required putting a hand in a cap.

### Why do golfers shout "fore" as a warning to those ahead of them?

When early cannons fired a barrage into enemy lines, over the heads of their own charging infantry, the shots were often imprecise. British artillery officers would shout, "Beware before" as a warning for their advancing troops to watch out for a misfired cannon ball. Over time, and in the heat of battle, "beware before" was abbreviated to "before," then eventually shortened to "fore," which found its way into golf as a warning that a volley was on its way.

### Why do we say we've been "stymied" when we are facing a difficult situation?

*Stymied* comes from the Scottish word *styme*, which means "unable to see," and its usage came from golf. A stymie was when a player's golf ball landed on the green directly between his opponent's ball and the hole, forcing the stymied player to either spin his ball around the other or hop over it with an iron. In 1951, a new rule allowed a golfer to mark the position and remove the obstructing ball for a putt.

### Why is Toronto's hockey team called the Maple Leafs?

In 1927, after having just been fired by the Rangers, Conn Smythe took the winnings from a horse race and bought the Toronto St. Pats hockey team, renaming them the Maple Leafs. Impressed with how brilliantly Canadians had fought in the First World War, Smythe named his new team after the soldiers' maple leaf insignia. Smythe is the man who said of hockey, "If you can't beat them in the alley, you can't beat them on the ice."

### Why is the Montreal hockey club called the "Habs," and what does their C.H. logo stand for?

The Montreal Canadiens began as an all–French Canadian hockey team that would be an honest representation of the Province of Quebec. Their nickname, the Habs, is an abbreviation of *les habitants*, meaning "those who live here." The C.H. logo on their sweaters stands for "Club de Hockey Canadien." The Canadiens won their first Stanley Cup in 1916, the year before the NHL was formed.

### Why are basketball players called "cagers"?

When Canadian James Naismith introduced basketball, the game was played with a soccer ball and the baskets were peach buckets nailed to the balcony at each end of the gym. The early games were rough and crude before Naismith introduced his thirteen rules in 1892 — so rough that the Trenton basketball team, playing in the first YMCA League, built a fence around the court to keep the ball in play. This fence was like a cage, and so the players were called cagers.

### How many coloured flags are used in auto racing, and what do they mean?

Seven flags are used as signals to drivers in car races: a green flag starts the race; a yellow flag means "don't pass"; a red flag means "stop for an emergency"; a black flag signals a rule infraction; a white flag indicates that the leaders are starting the last lap; a blue flag with a diagonal stripe tells slower cars to move aside; and finally the checkered flag means the race is over.

### Who is featured on the world's most valuable baseball card?

The most valuable baseball card in history was issued in 1909 and features Honus Wagner. One in mint condition sold for $110,000 in 1988. The reason it became so valuable is its scarcity — it was issued by the Sweet Caporal Cigarette Company, but Wagner, an eight-time National League batting champion, had it discontinued because he didn't want to promote smoking among children.

### What number has been retired by every Major League Baseball team and why?

In 1997, fifty years after he broke the colour barrier, every Major League Baseball team retired Jackie Robinson's number 42. Active players who had the number before 1997 were allowed to wear it until their retirement, but no other player will be able to wear the number again.

### What does the sign "No Pepper" mean at a baseball park?

The sign "No Pepper" is seen in many baseball dugouts and refers to a game played to warm up the players. During pepper, one player bunts grounders and hits line drives to a group of infielders standing about twenty feet away. The fielders play the ball then throw it back to the batter as quickly as possible, and he then attempts to hit those return throws. Pepper is banned when spectators are in the park for fear of injury.

### What are the seven different ways a baseball batter can reach first base?

In baseball, a batter can reach first base with a hit, or by being walked with four balls. He also goes to first if he is struck by a pitch or if the catcher interferes with his at bat. If the catcher drops the ball on strike three or the pitcher throws the ball out of the playing area the batter moves to first. Finally, the seventh way a batter can get on base is if the baseball becomes stuck in the umpire's mask or equipment.

### Why do the New York Yankees wear pinstripe baseball uniforms?

In 1925, thirty-year-old Babe Ruth was suffering from an intestinal disorder, and his weight ballooned to over 260 pounds. This embarrassed Yankees owner Jacob Rupert so much that he ordered the team to wear pinstripe uniforms in order to make the Bambino look thinner. Limited to 98 games that season because of surgery and suspensions, Babe Ruth still managed to hit .290 with 25 home runs.

## Why is the warm-up area for baseball pitchers called a "bullpen"?

As early as 1809, the term *bullpen* referred to a stockade for holding criminals. In the 1870s, a roped-off area in the outfield for standing room was nicknamed the bullpen by the *Cincinnati Enquirer*. When relief pitchers were introduced into the game they took over that area to warm up, and in a stroke of brilliance the Bull Durham Tobacco Company erected a sign overhead to confirm it as the bullpen.

## Why is there a seventh-inning stretch during a baseball game?

While attending a baseball game in 1910, American President William Howard Taft stood up to stretch his legs between the top and bottom of the seventh inning. The crowd stood out of respect because they thought the president was leaving, then as he sat back down so did the crowd, and a tradition was born. The stretch became popular with vendors because it was a last chance to sell off their hot dogs and French fries before fans started drifting home.

### What is the origin of the mascot?

A mascot brings good luck, and the name comes from *masco*, Latin for "witch." Primitive peoples believed that every tribe descended from a separate species of animal, which they recognized as their ancestors from what they hoped were their own characteristics of bravery and ferocity. It's the same reason most sporting teams name themselves after something they respect, hoping to attain the qualities of the Tigers, Indians, or even Mighty Ducks.

### Why was the Cleveland football team named the Browns?

Football franchises move around, and it was the Rams who represented Cleveland before moving to L.A. and then to St. Louis. In 1946, when the city was given a franchise in the AAFC, they held a contest to name the new team, and the winner was the Brown Bombers, after the great champion Joe Louis. However, the name was colour sensitive for the time, and so they compromised by naming the team the Browns after coach Paul Brown.

### What does *carte blanche* have to do with the name of the San Diego Chargers?

The naming of the San Diego football team had nothing to do with a military or an electrical charge. The team was named by the original owner, Barron Hilton, who called them the Chargers after a credit card. Hilton also owned the Carte Blanche credit card. Although to us *carte blanche* might be "white card," to the French it means "blank sheet," to be used like a blank cheque ... preferably to include a ticket to watch the San Diego Chargers.

### What does a football player's number tell you about his position?

American football introduced numbers in 1915 and names in 1961, but in 1967, numbers began indicating a player's position and eligibility. Quarterbacks and kickers wear 1 to 19, running and defensive backs 20 to 49, centres and linebackers 50 to 59, guards 60 to 69, tackles 70 to 79, and finally ends and defensive linemen wear between 60 and 89.

## Why is a horse race sometimes called a "derby"?

In England it's properly called a "darby," but everywhere else, including here, it's known as a "derby." In 1780, the twelfth Earl of Derby was having dinner with his friend Sir Charles Bunbury when they decided to sponsor a horse race for three-year-olds in Surrey, England. They tossed a coin to decide after which of them the race would be named and Derby won — otherwise the most exciting two minutes in sports would be the Kentucky Bunbury.

## Why is an obstacle-filled horse race called a "steeplechase"?

In early England, the church was the centre of a town's existence and was usually the largest and most prominent structure. For travellers on horseback, the first sign of their destination was the lofty church steeple rising above the trees. To the tired traveller, the sight was exhilarating and inspired the horsemen to quicken their paces, very often racing to see who could arrive at the steeple first. From this, a horse race became known as a "steeplechase."

## Why are legal issues, basketball games, and tennis tournaments all settled on a "court"?

Like *courtesy*, the word *court* evolved from the Latin words *cum*, meaning "together," and *hortus*, the derivative of *horticulture* — so a court was an enclosed garden where young boys of noble birth learned proper social conduct. In both the judicial and sporting sense a court is a specified area within which you are expected to practise courtesy while respecting authority.

### Why is Canada's national sport called "lacrosse"?

*Lacrosse*, "the little brother of war," was considered good training for Native American warriors. Teams consisting of hundreds of players often involved entire villages in brutal contests that could last as long as three days. To the French explorers who were the first Europeans to see the game, the stick resembled a bishop's ceremonial staff, called a "crozier," surmounted by a cross, or *la crosse* — and the sport had a new name.

### Why do we use the word *checkmate* to end a game of chess?

The game of chess, played by two players, each trying to capture the other's king with a sixteen-piece army of horses, foot soldiers, chariots, and elephants, surfaced in India in around 500 B.C. The game was adopted first by the Persians and then by the Arabs, who introduced it to Europe during their conquest of Spain. The Persian word for king is *shah*. *Checkmate* is from the Arabic *Shah mat*, which literally means "the king is dead."

### Why is a small sporting facility called a "gymnasium" while a larger one is a "stadium"?

The word *gymnasium* is from the Greek word *gymnos*, which means "nude." Thus, *gymnasium* literally means "a school for naked exercise." The first Olympic event for the nude male athletes, or gymnasts, was a foot race known as a *stade*, which was a Greek unit of measurement for the distance of the race (which was six hundred feet), and that is why the facility was called a stadium.

# POLITICS & THE MILITARY

### Why are governmental and legal delays called "red tape"?

English monarchs used to write legal decrees on rolls of parchment and then bind them up with red silk ribbons. To give their work an important appearance, government bureaucrats copied the "red tape" practice. Not to be outdone, lawyers followed with ribbons of their own. The expression took hold after Charles Dickens described the frustration of dealing with governmental and legal bungling as "cutting through red tape."

### Where did the sarcastic phrase "Bob's your uncle" come from?

"Bob's your uncle" is a common British phrase and now means that you've accomplished something without much effort. It originated in 1887 when Prime Minister Robert Cecil appointed his nephew, Arthur Balfour, chief secretary for Ireland. The public was outraged at this blatant act of nepotism and began using "Bob's your uncle" to describe any situation where favouritism influenced the outcome.

### Why is political favouritism called "pork barrel politics"?

Long before refrigeration, North American farmers kept supplies of salt pork stored in barrels, and the amount of meat on hand indicated the family's prosperity. If the barrel was low on pork, it meant the possibility of disaster through starvation. When a politician sought and gained favouritism for his constituents, he was said to have filled the pork barrels of those who had elected him, thereby assuring his re-election.

### Why do we call someone seeking political office a "candidate"?

In ancient Rome, someone seeking election would appear in public wearing a white robe to symbolize his pure character. *Candidate* comes from *candidatus*, meaning a man wearing pure white. Not fooled by the white toga, the Romans said that politicians needed to make three fortunes while in office: the first to pay back the money borrowed to buy votes, the second to bribe officials when eventually tried for misconduct, and the third for retirement.

## Why is someone who exposes political corruption called a "muckraker"?

When President Teddy Roosevelt called the reporters who exposed political and corporate corruption "muckrakers," the term caught on and is now used to describe tabloid journalism. *Muck* is manure, and the word was borrowed from John Bunyons's book *Pilgrim's Progress*, wherein a man — even though he had been promised a celestial crown — constantly kept his eyes and his muck rake on the filth of the floor instead of looking only to his halo.

## Why are armoured battle vehicles called "tanks"?

In ancient India, large pits were dug to collect the monsoon rains and were called *tanken*. In the seventeenth century the concept was brought home to Britain and was introduced in English as "tank," a place to store water. In 1915, when the British designed a heavily armoured combat vehicle, they built them under the cover of building water tanks and shipped them to the front in crates marked "Tanks." They were introduced at the Battle of the Somme.

## Why doesn't an "ovation" signify a "triumph"?

A *triumph* was a Roman celebration of a military victory over an enemy of the state. The victorious commander rode a chariot in a grand parade with his entire army and the booty and slaves he had won. An *ovation* was a less elaborate honour for a general who had won victory without bloodshed, perhaps by treaty or reason. He was denied a chariot and either walked or rode a horse during a less imposing ceremony.

## Why do we say "deep six" when we mean to eliminate or destroy something?

During the Watergate scandals, John Dean said that John Erlichman told him to shred some sensitive documents and then deep six the briefcase by throwing it into the river. "By the deep six" is a nautical term referring to sounding the water's depth and means six fathoms (eleven metres or thirty-six feet). In the navy, to deep six something meant to dispose of an item by tossing it overboard into deep water where it couldn't be found.

## Why is an all-out fight called a "pitched battle"?

One of the meanings of the word *pitch* is "to set things in order." For example, when you pitch a tent, you are using a military expression for lining up the tents in rows. Unlike a skirmish or a surprise attack, a pitched battle was one in which the two sides lined up in formation facing each other until the order was given for the carnage to begin. The two disciplined sides held their ranks as they approached and then met each other in what was called a pitched battle.

## Why are foot soldiers called "infantry"?

The word *soldier* is from the Latin word *solidus*, meaning a gold coin, because it cost money to raise an army of mercenaries. The word *infantry* is from *infant*, with a Latin derivative meaning "non speaking," because, like children, well-disciplined soldiers never talk back or challenge orders. Curiously, another use of the word *soldier* is in reference to an army ant, due to the fact that other than humans, ants are the only creatures on earth to go into battle in formation.

### Why do we say that a guilty person must "face the music"?

To "face the music" comes from the military "drumming out" ceremony for disgraced soldiers. This ritual called for only drums to accompany the dishonoured as he was stripped of his rank and colours in front of his assembled unit. For cavalrymen, this humiliation was enhanced by having the offender sit backwards on his horse so that while leaving he could still see, as well as hear, the drums and the band. He was forced to face the music.

### Why is someone who doesn't live up to expectations called a "flash in the pan"?

On a pioneer flintlock rifle the hammer struck a flint to create a spark that ignited a small amount of priming powder in what was called the pan. This ignition then set off the main charge of gunpowder, causing a small explosion that fired the bullet through the barrel. When the powder in the pan didn't ignite properly it created a flash, but the rifle wouldn't fire. It looked good, but it was only a "flash in the pan."

### Why is a single-minded person said to be "zeroed in"?

Before the modern era, rifle gunsights were aligned to hit a target at a known distance. Therefore, with the guesswork removed, any adjustment from a set position would be zero. The same principle applies to artillery batteries, which adjust their fire to a fixed point or "ground zero," a term still used with satellite- and laser-guided bombs and missiles. Like the single-minded person, they're zeroed in.

### Where does the disciplinary order "toe the line" come from?

"Toe the line" is the same as "toe the mark" and means "follow the rules or pay the consequences." In many sports, such as foot racing, the athletes were required to stand with their toes against a scratched line to ensure a fair start. As punishment in the navy, no matter what the weather, young trainees were forced to stand for hours with their toes touching a seam on the ship's deck, and this too was toeing the line.

### Why when waking up do we say, "Rise and shine" or "Shake a leg"?

"Rise and shine" comes from a 1916 United States Marine Corps manual that instructed noncommissioned officers to enter the privates' barracks in the early morning and use the phrase to wake the men. While *rise* means "get up," *shine* means "make sure your boots and brass are ready for inspection." The Royal Navy used "shake a leg" to warn any women who might be sleeping in a hammock to show a leg or suffer the embarrassment of being rousted with the men.

### Why is the control area of an aircraft called a "cockpit"?

When the hideous sport of cockfighting was legal, the birds were taken to a pit in the ground where they fought to the death. These fights were quick and bloody, and for this reason, the "cockpit" became the designated name of the room on a warship were surgeons attended the wounded and dying. During the First World War, pilots, like the roosters, were inserted into a confined space to do battle, and so they named that space the cockpit.

### Why did First World War fighter pilots wear long silk scarves?

The dashing image of First World War fighter pilots wearing long silk scarves had nothing to do with fashion. The open-cockpit biplanes were very primitive with no rear-view mirror, so the pilot depended entirely on his own vision to avoid or mount an attack. The scarf was used to wipe grease from his goggles and to keep his neck from chafing against his collar as he constantly turned his head while watching for the enemy.

## How did a telegram bring the United States into the First World War?

In 1917, the British intercepted a cable from the German foreign minister to their Mexican ambassador proposing an alliance whereby the Mexicans would reacquire Texas, Arizona, and New Mexico if that country would join Germany in an attack from the south on the neutral Americans. The British made the telegram public on March 1, and the outcry forced the United States into the war a month later.

## What orbital advantage did Cape Canaveral have to cause NASA to choose the Florida location for its first space launches?

Cape Canaveral was chosen as a launch site not only because NASA needed the booster rockets to fall harmlessly into the ocean but also, and more importantly, because the earth moves from west to east at 910 miles an hour. This Florida location allowed them to fire a rocket to the east with an added velocity push of 17,300 miles an hour from the spinning of the earth.

## What was the cost in human life to liberate each Kuwaiti citizen during Operation Desert Storm?

After Saddam Hussein invaded Kuwait, an American-led military force liberated the tiny country in 1991 — but at what cost? There were 491,000 Kuwaiti citizens, who made up only 28 percent of the country's population. The rest, or 72 percent, were immigrant labourers. Estimates are that 150,000 Iraqis were killed during the war, while 141 American, 18 British, 2 French, and 44 Arab soldiers gave their lives. This means it cost one life to liberate every three Kuwaitis.

## Why does "sally forth" mean to go forward with a new venture?

Today it implies less danger, but to "sally forth" was originally a military term meaning to suddenly rush forward. The Latin derivation of *sally* is *salire*, meaning "to leap." Castles and fortresses had closely guarded openings in the walls designed for mounting a quick counterattack against a siege. These were called sally ports, from which the defenders would vigorously rush, or sally forth, into battle.

## What is the meaning of the battle cry "Give no quarter"?

In battle, to give no quarter means to take no prisoners. In this case, the word *quarter* has no numerical value but rather refers to the antiquated use of the word for a dwelling place or area, such as the Latin Quarter or a soldier's living quarters or barracks. To grant or give quarter would mean to show mercy and provide prisoners with shelter. "No quarter asked and no quarter given" means this is a fight to the death.

## Why do we say, "Lock and load" when preparing for the inevitable?

The expression "lock and load" comes from American G.I.s during the Second World War and refers to loading the M1 rifle for imminent combat. The phrase means to insert a full ammunition clip into the rifle, then lock the bolt forward, forcing a round into the chamber ready to fire. The original order was "load and lock," but after John Wayne reversed the order to "lock and load" in *The Sands of Iwo Jima*, the expression stuck.

## Why are military guards, some garden fences, and people on strike all called "pickets"?

A picket line, of course, is a group of union people exercising their right to protest, while a military picket is a guard on duty to protect the perimeter of an encampment. The word *picket* comes from the early French settlers, who made fortified stockades from sharpened tree trunks, which they called *piquet*, meaning "pointed sticks." It lives on in the pointed slats of picket fences and in the actions of union strikers.

# SHIPS & SAILING

## Why does "jury-rigged" mean a temporary repair with whatever is at hand?

In the seventeenth century, when a ship's mast was damaged at sea, a "jury mast" was rigged to hold the sail until the replacement could be found. Because this was a critical situation the repairs had to be done within a day, or in French *un jour*, which in this case is the origin of *jury*. Something jury-rigged is a temporary repair and has nothing to do with "jerry-built," which means permanent bad work.

## Why would you give a "swashbuckler" or a bully a "wide berth"?

*Swashbuckler*, a word we use for a pirate, was created from the archaic words *swash*, meaning "to make noise by striking," and *buckler*, meaning "shield." A swaggering brute yelling and banging his sword on his shield was called a swashbuckler. These bullies were given a "wide berth," which in nautical lingo means to anchor or berth a ship a safe distance away from another that might cause trouble.

## Why do we say that someone is "on the spot" when they're facing big trouble?

To be "on the spot" means you're in serious difficulty, and it comes from the pirates of the Caribbean. The "spot" is the ace of spades, a card that pirates ceremoniously showed to a condemned person indicating that he was about to be executed as a traitor. To be put on the spot has become much less dire, and instead of being a signal that you're being put to death, it has evolved into meaning, "Explain yourself or you're out of here."

## Why do we say that someone arrogant needs to be "taken down a peg"?

A ship's colours are raised or lowered to signal the ship's status. "All flags flying" signals great pride, but flags could also indicate degrees between failure and conquest. These flags were once held in place by a system of pegs, so lowering them was done by taking down a peg. This was a shame to the ship and its crew and gave us the expression for humiliation: to be taken down a peg.

### What's the origin of the expression "son of a gun"?

Early in the eighteenth century, wives and girlfriends (as well as the occasional prostitute) were allowed to go to sea with the sailors during long voyages. When one of them became pregnant and was about to give birth at sea, a canvas curtain was placed near the midship gun where the birth would take place. If the newborn's father was in doubt, and it often was, the birth was registered in the log as the "son of a gun."

### How did "spick and span" come to mean very clean?

Today, Spick and Span is a trade name for a well-known cleanser, but the expression began in the fourteenth century as the nautical term "spick and span new," to describe a freshly built or refurbished ship. A *spick* was a spike, while *span* was a Viking reference to new wood, but also means any distance between two extremities (such as the bow and stern of a ship). The wooden ship was so clean that even the spikes looked new.

### Why does "chewing the fat" mean gossip or casual conversation?

During the twentieth century, "chewing the fat" came to mean passing time with informal small talk. The phrase originated with the grumbling of nineteenth-century British sailors whose lean diet was often nothing more than the fat from barrels of salt pork. Their whining while chewing the tough meat would expand to include complaints about every other hardship at sea and became known as "chewing the fat."

**Why do we say that someone who has overcome an obstacle with ease has passed with "flying colours"?**

Since the eighteenth century, ships of the navy have used flags to communicate their status or well-being. The most prominent flag, of course, is that of the ship's country, but there are dozens of other banners, which are called "colours." The most elaborate use of this bunting is after a victory at sea, when a triumphant ship returns to its home port with a proud and full display of flying colours.

**Why do we describe something approximate as "by and large"?**

In early sailing jargon, *by* was "by the wind," and when a helmsman was ordered to fill the sails he was told to steer "full and by." This required great skill and was called steering small. A less experienced helmsman might have been told to steer large with the order "by and large," which meant use the wind but don't fill the sails. This is how "by and large" came to mean not quite true, but close enough.

**If you're short of cash why might you ask for a loan to "tide you over"?**

If you ask for money to tide you over, you are using a nautical term to reassure the lender that repayment is inevitable. When a boat or ship wants to enter a river from the ocean at low tide, its way will be blocked by the accumulation of mud or sand that has been swept downstream and collected at the mouth of the river. When the predictable tide rises and the obstacle is "tided over" the boat, like a borrower, can continue its progress.

**Why do we say that something lost has "gone by the board"?**

During the time of wooden ships, sailors often referred to their sailing vessel as "the Boards." We still use their language when we board a ship or are on board as part of a crew. *Outboard* is outside the boat, while *inboard* is inside. When a sailing ship's mast was broken by enemy cannon or in a storm and couldn't be salvaged, the captain would order the ropes holding it to be cut, letting it drift away or "go by the board."

## Why is a severe labour dispute called a "strike"?

Conditions on board commercial sailing ships were miserable. On long voyages, food and water went bad and hygienic conditions were lower than for animals in a stable. If they suspected that a ship was poorly prepared, it wasn't uncommon for the crew to strike the main sail, making it impossible to go to sea until conditions improved. This gave us the word *strike* to describe any extreme action by labour against management.

# HOLIDAYS

## Why is Easter a higher Christian holiday than Christmas?

With the rise of Christianity, the church decided that death days were the real birthdays because the deceased was being reborn in paradise, and so the date of a person's demise was recorded as their birth, or rebirth, day. The birthdays of saints are celebrated on their death days. It was through this logic that Christ's death day, or Easter, became more important than Christmas.

## Why is Thanksgiving celebrated six and a half weeks earlier in Canada than in the United States?

It took two hundred years after the pilgrims first celebrated Thanksgiving in 1621 before it became an annual holiday in the U.S. It was Sarah Hale, the author of "Mary Had a Little Lamb," who convinced Abraham Lincoln to create the annual celebration in 1863. Canada went along in 1879, but because of a shorter growing season changed the date in 1957 from the end of November to the second Monday in October.

## Why are Christmas songs called "carols"?

A Christmas carol is a song of religious joy, but the musical form of a carol doesn't have to include Christmas. Its main feature is the repetition, either musically or chorally, of a theme, as in a circle. The word *carole* entered English from the French at the end of the thirteenth century, but it's much older than that. Originally, a carole was a ring dance where men and women held hands while dancing and singing in a circle.

## How did turkey become the traditional Christmas dinner?

Up until the nineteenth century, mincemeat pie was the common Christmas feast in both North America and Europe, with preferred birds

being pigeon, peacock, guinea hen, and goose. Turkey was introduced from America to Europe by the Spanish in the sixteenth century and caught on big time in 1843 after Ebenezer Scrooge sent a turkey to Bob Cratchet in the Charles Dickens story *A Christmas Carol.*

**What are we saying when we sing "Deck the Halls with Boughs of Holly"?**

The middle Dutch word *decken* meant "to cover or adorn" and came from *dec*, which originally meant any cover, such as a tarpaulin or a roof, and was borrowed into English as a nautical term in the fifteenth century. Although today a backyard deck might mean a wooden patio, a ship's deck was not a floor but a roof to cover cannons. The Christmas carol "Deck the Halls" is saying simply "cover the walls" with boughs of holly.

## Why do we kiss under the mistletoe?

Two centuries before Christ's birth, the Druids celebrated the winter solstice with mistletoe because it enhanced fertility and was a favourite of the gods. The Romans hung it prominently during orgies, which is how it became associated with kissing and also why the church banned it in the fourth century. The name *mistletoe* is from the Germanic word *mista*, meaning "manure" or "dung," because the plant grows out of oak trees well-fertilized by bird droppings.

## How did holly become associated with Christmas?

No one knows the exact date of Christ's birth, although May 30 is the most popular scholastic guess. December 25 was chosen early in the fourth century in an effort to convert those of other religions who celebrated the winter solstice. Holly was a prominent part of pre-Christian winter celebrations and was used to bring others into the fold by using its leaves to symbolize a crown of thorns and its red berries to symbolize Christ's blood at the crucifixion.

## What happened to the man who outlawed Christmas?

In 1643, the English Puritan parliament frowned on the pagan rituals of Christmas and banned its celebration after William Prynne published his anti-Christmas manifesto. Clergymen were imprisoned for so much as preaching on December 25. After several years of rioting against the ban, King Charles II arrested Prynne and had him pilloried then had both his ears cut off while the manifesto was burned in front of him. The king re-established Christmas celebrations, but not before having Prynne expelled from Oxford and the legal profession.

## What is the origin of the New Year's song *Auld Lang Syne*?

The tone and lyrics of *Auld Lang Syne* seem to capture perfectly the emotions involved in the passing of the fleeting accomplishments and losses of one calendar year coinciding with the rise of hope in a new one. *Auld lang syne* is Scottish and literally means "old long since," or, in modern language, simply "long ago." The song was written down by the poet Robert Burns, but he wasn't the composer. Burns heard the folk song being sung by an anonymous old man and copied it down before passing it on to become a ceremonial fixture of New Year's Eve.

# BELIEFS & SUPERSTITIONS

## What is the curse on the Hope diamond?

The Hope diamond is a steel blue, forty-four-and-a-half-carat, walnut-sized diamond that is supposedly cursed, since it was stolen from the statue of a Hindu god in 1642. Since then, its owners, including Marie Antoinette, have all had brushes with madness and violent death. It's named after a British banking family who were financially ruined. It's now at the Smithsonian Institute and is owned by the government of the United States of America.

## What is the origin of the Tooth Fairy?

The ritual of placing a baby tooth under the pillow to be replaced overnight with money from the Tooth Fairy is a compilation of several European customs. In Venice an old witch did the job, while in France the Virgin Mary traded money and sometimes candy for children's teeth. Other cultures buried the tooth, or threw it at the sun for favours from the gods. The fairy was of course an Irish innovation and took hold in North America during the middle of the ninetenth century.

## Why is a rabbit's foot considered good luck?

If you realize that primitive societies couldn't tell the difference between a rabbit and a hare, then you'll understand this ancient logic as to why the rabbit's foot is a symbol of good luck. Hares are born with their eyes open, giving them knowledge of prenatal life. The rabbit burrows underground and shares secrets with the underworld. Finally, both animals' incredible fertility could be shared by carrying the rabbit's foot as a phallus of good luck.

## Why do some people believe black cats are bad luck?

If you believe that a black cat crossing your path is bad luck, you believe in witchcraft. Legend has its that in the 1560s in England, a father and son threw stones at a cat that had startled them on a moonless night. The wounded cat ran into the nearby home of a suspected witch. The next day the old woman was seen in public limping and bruised, and a superstition was born which caused the burning alive of innocent women in the seventeenth century.

**Did the near tragedy of Apollo 13 cause the NASA scientists to become superstitious?**

Apollo 13 was launched on the eleventh of the fourth month in the seventieth year of that century. One plus one plus four plus seven plus zero totals thirteen. Liftoff was at 13:13 central military time, and the explosion took place on the thirteenth day of April. NASA claims no superstition — but has never again used the number thirteen on a manned space flight.

### How did astrology connect the lives of Winston Churchill, Franklin Roosevelt, and Charlie Chaplin with that of Adolf Hitler?

Chaplin and Hitler were associated astrologically from birth, because both men were born within the same hour in the same week of the same year. The date connecting Churchill and FDR with the German dictator is January 30. It's the date of President Roosevelt's birth, Winston Churchill's death, and Hitler's ascension to power in Germany.

### Why is breaking a mirror considered seven years of bad luck?

Before glass was introduced in 1300 A.D., manufactured mirrors were simply polished metal. Around 6 B.C., in much the same manner one would now use as a crystal ball, the Greeks began practising fortune-telling from a subject's reflected image in a bowl of water. If, during a reading, the bowl with the image fell and broke it meant disaster. The Romans limited the curse to seven years because they believed that's how long it took for human life to renew itself.

### Why does a bad day mean that you got up on the "wrong side of the bed"?

For centuries, to be left-handed was considered evil. Ancient Egyptians drew all the good armies as being right-handed, while the enemies were lefties. Until only recently left-handed children were forced to learn to use their right hands in school. The word *ambidextrous* means two right hands. Getting up on the wrong side of the bed means your left foot touched the floor first, signalling that you were open to dark influences.

### Why is it bad luck to open an umbrella indoors?

The umbrella is an ancient African innovation and was intended as a portable shade against the sun. After entering Europe through Spain in the twelfth century it became more valuable as a protection from the rain. The superstition of bad luck if opened indoors came from the African belief that to open an umbrella in the shade was an insult to the sun god and would cause him to bring down his wrath on the offender.

### When someone we are discussing shows up, why do we say, "Speak of the Devil"?

When someone recently mentioned in a conversation suddenly turns up we might say, "Speak of the Devil" as though our conversation has brought the subject into our midst. This is precisely what the expression means, because in the Middle Ages it was believed that any mention of the Devil would be an invitation for the evil one to appear either in spirit or in action, and so other than within ecclesiastical circles, his name was avoided at all costs.

### Why is happiness referred to as "seventh heaven" or "cloud nine"?

The ancient Jews believed that the highest heaven, or "heaven of heavens," and the home of God and his chosen angels was the seventh heaven. The Moslems agreed that the seventh heaven was the pinnacle of ecstasy. "Cloud nine" was coined by the U.S. weather bureau and means "as high as clouds can get," or between thirty and forty thousand feet. Its meaning as a euphoric state came about in the 1950s.

### Why do we say that someone going nowhere is in "limbo"?

To be in limbo means nothing is happening, neither good nor bad. Because the Christian church believed that only those "born again" could enter heaven they needed an afterlife destination for the other good souls. Limbo is the rim of hell and the destination for the right-eous who died before the coming of Christ as well as infants, unbelievers, and the unbaptized. Limbo is a place without glory or pain.

### Why are ministers of the gospel called "Reverend," "Pastor," or "Parson"?

*Reverend* first appeared in seventeenth-century England and is derived from the Latin *reverendus*, meaning "worthy of respect." *Pastor* is from the Latin word for shepherd, which is how Christ referred to himself. On the other hand, *parson* comes from New England, where because the minister was one of the few who could read or write they called him "the town person," which in the local accent became "the town parson."

### Why is the Pontiff of the Roman Catholic Church called the "Pope," and where is the "Holy See"?

In Italian, the word *pope* is an endearment meaning "father" or "papa." The responsibility of the leader of the Roman Catholic Church is to build bridges between God and mankind, and the title *Pontiff* is from the original Roman reference *pontifex*, meaning "bridge builder." The Holy See is a corruption of "Holy seat," or throne, and refers to the place where this throne is housed.

**Why when someone receives an unfair judgment do we say they've been given a "short shrift"?**

*Shrift* is an ancient word and comes from the act of shriving, which is the confessional process conducted by a priest. In his pursuit of forgiveness, a confessor seeks absolution for the sins of his soul through a process of penance administered by the priest. A short shrift refers to the brief time allowed with a priest to a condemned convict just before his execution.

WORDS

## Why do we say that a subordinate person is "kowtowing" to another when they are "knuckling under" to their wishes?

We call the finger joints *knuckles*, but the word used to mean any joint in the body, including the elbows and knees. To "knuckle under" is left over from those days and refers to bending your knees or bowing, signalling submission. *Kowtow* is Chinese and means "to kneel and press your forehead to the ground," which was expected in the presence of the emperor or anyone else you feared.

## Why when someone has been banished or ostracized by a group do we say they've been "blackballed"?

*Ostracize* comes from a Greek word meaning "voting tablet," and the ritual of "blackballing" someone was a democratic process of elimination. A group decided if a suspect member would be banished or allowed to stay by dropping black and white balls into a ballot box. The word *ballot* means "little ball." If the majority were black, the candidate lost and was said to have been blackballed.

## Why when we hurt our elbow do we say we've hit our "funny bone"?

When we strike our elbow, although it's no laughing matter, we say that the tingling sensation is from our funny bone. In fact, the prickling discomfort comes from striking the ulnar nerve, and the word *funny* comes from some scholar with a sense of humour who turned the whole thing into a pun during the nineteenth century. The ulnar nerve passes over the end of the humerus, which inspired the term "funny bone."

## Why is a small newspaper called a "gazette"?

In 59 B.C. Julius Caesar introduced the first handwritten daily newspapers, which were posted in prominent locations around Rome. However, it wasn't until long after Gutenberg's printing press was invented that news became an industry. During the mid-sixteenth century, citizens of Venice paid to hear public readings of the news, and the price was a small copper Italian coin called a *gazetta*, which gave us the word *gazette* for a newspaper.

**Why when asking for a loan might you say you need a "stake" to carry you over?**

Asking for a stake means you need to see money to continue with a project. The expression comes from the early days of bare-knuckle boxing, when promoters often stiffed the fighters by absconding with the gate money before the count of ten. To ensure that they'd be paid, boxers insisted that their share of the money be placed in a pouch on a stake near the ring, where they could see it during the bout. This was known as stake money.

**Why are both the contents of a novel and the level of a building referred to as a "story"?**

The Latin word *historia* entered English as *history*, meaning an account of significant events. By the sixteenth century the abbreviated *story* took the meaning of an imaginative narrative. In the Middle Ages, by using sculpture and stained glassed windows, architects told themes from history on the fronts of large buildings, each being the height of one of the building's floors. Each floor told a story.

**Why do we say we've been "upstaged" when someone else grabs all the attention?**

To be upstaged now means to lose due credit to a lesser person. In the theatre, "upstage" refers to the back of the stage, which at one time was built higher than the front. This was because the theatre floor was flat, and a slanted stage gave a better view of all the actors. Plays were crafted placing noble characters at the rear (where they appeared higher and more regal) even though they might have fewer lines than the others.

### Why is a crowning achievement called a "masterpiece"?

"Masterpiece" suggests great art, but when the word first appeared in German as *meisterstuck*, it referred to a medieval standard of excellence expected from an apprentice before being allowed to join a guild of master craftsmen. After many years under the guidance of a master, the apprentice submitted a piece of work for assessment. If his work or masterpiece passed the test, he would be allowed into the trade as a master craftsman.

### If "right" means correct, does "left" mean incorrect?

The word *right* surfaced in English as *riht* and meant "straight." To put things right is to straighten them out. *Right* took the metaphorical meaning of "good" or "just," as in the Bill of Rights, because most people were right-handed. The suggestion that *left* is incorrect was understood, like in a "left-handed compliment," which is an insult. *Right* became a synonym for correct, but *left* was evil and so was left alone.

### What's the origin of the word *window*?

Early Norse homes were simply designed and often included a stable area for livestock under the same roof as the humans. In the winter, because the tightly shut doors trapped stale air and smoke from the indoor fires, they built holes high on the walls and in the roof for ventilation. They called these openings *vindr auga*, which means "the wind's eye." When the British copied this practice they modified *wind's eye* to *window*.

## Why is a "benchmark" used as a reference point for quality and precision?

A *benchmark* is a surveyor's term and, beginning in the nineteenth century, meant a mark cut into a stone or a wall that established the exact level of altitude for a tract of land they were measuring. Today a benchmark is a high standard to strive for, but the surveyors took their meaning from the word *bench* as it relates to a long tract of level elevated land along a shoreline or a sloping hill.

## Why do we say that someone tricked has been "hoodwinked"?

To have been hoodwinked means to have been put at a disadvantage. The term derives from early children's games like Pin the Tail on the Donkey and Blind Man's Bluff, where someone was either blindfolded or hooded and required to complete a task without being able to see. Muggers also employed the hood to blind and rob innocent victims on the street. *Wink* was really a half-wink, a reference to the blind point when the eye is covered by the lid.

## Why is someone who doesn't drink alcohol called a "tee-totaller"?

An 1846 tombstone in Preston, England, has the inscription, "Beneath this stone are deposited the remains of Richard Turner, author of the word 'TeeTotal.'" Turner emphasized the "T" to stress the first letter in *total*. Another group filled out pledges with a letter after their signature to reflect their positions: "M" for moderation, "A" for abstinence, and "T" for total abstinence.

## Why is a disaster called a "fiasco"?

The word *fiasco* is Italian for an ordinary flask or bottle and comes from the opera, where audiences would greet a false note or a bad performance with the cry "Ola fiasco." The logic was that they had come to hear perfection but were getting a second-rate performance, and so just as a glass blower's flawed attempt at a beautiful piece of art was discarded or assigned to be a common flask, the opera was second rate, like a fiasco.

**How did the word *okay* come to mean all right?**

The word *okay* (or O.K.) is American and surfaced for the first time in the *Boston Morning Post* on March 23, 1839. It was a comedic use of "All Correct" and was deliberately misspelled as "Oll Korrect," which when abbreviated becomes the letters O.K. The abbreviation caught on around Boston and New York and became a slogan for President Martin Van Buren's campaign for re-election.

**How did the word *halo* come to mean divinity?**

The word *halo* is Greek and literally means "threshing floor," because it described the circular track followed by a team of oxen while threshing golden coloured grain. The idea of the halo has pagan roots and wasn't accepted by the Christian church until the seventh century. Its symbolism of heavenly authority is the reason monarchs wear crowns and Native chiefs wear bonnets of feathers. In religious paintings a halo suggests a sacred aura.

**Why is something tasteless said to be "tawdry"?**

In 672 A.D., the eventual St. Audrey entered a convent for a life of penance and prayer. As a young woman she had worn fine necklaces, a habit she now considered the cause of her terminal neck tumour, which she covered with a scarf. After her death, women honoured her by wearing fine silk St. Audrey scarves, which through time were followed by cheap imitations for the English lower classes, who pronounced "St. Audrey" as "tawdry."

## Why are a vocal restraint and a joke both called a "gag"?

The original meaning of *gag* was to prevent someone from speaking, either by covering the mouth or through a legal restraint such as a gag order. The jocular use of *gag* originated in the theatre to describe times when an actor inserted an unscripted, and often humorous, line into a play. It was called a gag because the ad lib often caused fellow actors to lose their focus and become speechless.

## Why kind of a job is created by "featherbedding"?

About sixty years ago, when a group of railroad men complained about being unable to sleep on their hard bunks, the boss asked, "What do you want … feather beds?" At the time a feather bed was the warmest and coziest place to curl up and sleep, and so companies began calling the union practice of creating unnecessary soft jobs requiring little or no work, for members who would otherwise be laid off, "featherbedding."

## How did the word *carnival* come to mean a self-indulgent celebration?

In the Christian calendar, Lent, a reverent and disciplined observance of Easter, begins on Ash Wednesday. In the Middle Ages the faithful were forbidden to eat meat during Lent, and so the day before Ash Wednesday became known as Fat Tuesday, when everyone would overindulge in a Mardi Gras of what was about to be forbidden. In Church Latin, *carne vale* literally means "farewell to meat."

## Why do we refer to a bad joke as being "corny"?

The reason a cheap joke is called "corny" comes from mail order seed catalogues from the early twentieth century. In an effort to make reading

I just flew in from New York

about seeds interesting, the publishers mixed in cartoons, jokes, and riddles throughout the crop and garden book. These inserts were of desperately low quality and were known as corn catalogue jokes, and were eventually simply called corny, which came to mean any failed attempt at entertainment.

## Why do we call a powerful earth-moving tractor a "bulldozer"?

"Bulldozer" is a metaphor that originated in the Deep South during Reconstruction. A "bull-dose" was a dose of the bullwhip and was used by American terrorist groups to inhibit freed black slaves from using their new mandate to vote. In 1925, when a machine appeared that could change everything in its path through sheer force, it took the name bulldozer from the bullwhip and changed the meaning of the word.

## Why is something of little value called "fluff" and poor workmanship called "shoddy"?

The word *shoddy* is used to describe both poor workmanship and poor character, while *fluff* means of little value. *Shoddy* is derived from *shode* meaning "shed" or "thrown off," and refers to the excess tossed from the good cloth during the process of weaving. This fluff is re-spun and used to make similar but cheaper wool products, which, although they look good, through time reveal their poor quality — they are fluff, of little value.

## Why do we ask for "the real dope" when we want the truth?

*Dope* is from the Dutch word *doop*, meaning a thick sauce, and became a drug term from the semi-liquid form of opium smoked by drug addicts. The use of *dope* meaning "stupid" came from the retarded behaviour of someone under the influence of the drug. The use of "the real dope" as information came in around 1900 when gamblers checking on racehorses needed to know whether or not any of the horses were drugged or doped.

## Why do we call a large quantity "a lot"?

It takes a lot of people to play a lottery or there won't be enough money to make the prize worthwhile. *Lot* is from the word *lottery*, a very ancient practice from a time when people cast marked pebbles into a pot and then selected a winner through a draw. To "throw in your lot" with the others meant you had joined them in the gamble. A lot, meaning a large quantity, took its meaning from the many balls or entrants in the lottery pool.

## Why when things go wrong do we say they've gone "haywire"?

Haywire is used on farms to hold together bales of hay. It's tightly bound and when cut will sometimes whip around in a dangerous, erratic manner. But more than this, because haywire is often used as a temporary repair on machinery that has broken down, or to hold together any equipment that's falling apart, it became a rural expression for things or people that aren't functioning properly ... they've gone haywire.

## Why is someone who has been defeated forced to say "uncle"?

Being forced to say "uncle" after losing a fight is a man thing and dates back to the late nineteenth century in the United States. In today's terms picture a chauvinistic Republican defeating a Libertarian in some form of physical combat. To the chauvinist, the highest order of submitting to decency is believing in the state, and so to stop the beating the defeated man must cry "Uncle Sam," which in time became "uncle."

## Why are the bundles of tissue fibres that move our bones called "muscles"?

In the average adult male body, there are forty-five pounds of bone compared to sixty-five pounds of muscle. The average female is 15 percent less. We call them muscles because when a Roman physician saw how they rippled under the skin when flexed, it reminded him of the skittering of a small mouse, or *musculus*, and so that's what he called them. En route to English, the small mouse *musculus* became *muscle*.

## Why are nightclothes called "pyjamas"?

In the sixteenth century, the first nightgowns appeared as loose-fitting, full-length unisex garments for warmth in bed. In the eighteenth century the negligee became a lounging garment for women while, the nightshirt with loose-fitting pants called pyjamas replaced the long gown for men. Pyjamas were modelled after harem pants and were imported from Iran, using the Persian words *pae* for leg garment and *jama* for clothing.

## Why is something obscene said to be "gross"?

Gross began as a prejudicial reference to those who are overweight, during the 1950s. *Gross* is from the Latin *grossus*, meaning thick or large, which in the fourteenth century gave us the word *grocer* for a wholesale merchant who bought and sold in large quantities. To an accountant, gross means "without deductions." To "gross out" in the broad sense, as in being disgusted by anything crude or excessive, took hold during the 1960s.

## Why do we use the word *neat*, as in "That was a neat idea?"

The word *neat*, although dated, is often used to describe something pleasing. It is also used to order a shot of alcohol straight from the bottle without any mix or ice, and it's within this context that the word became popular. The original meaning of *neat* was to describe anything clean or undiluted, without any impurities. This gave us the extension of meaning tidy, as in a teenager keeping a neat room, which is a neat idea.

## Why do we say we have a "yen" for something that we crave?

Although a yen is also a type of Japanese currency, that meaning has nothing to do with an overwhelming urge; instead, the yen in question is from the Cantonese Chinese *yin-yan*. *Yin* means opium, and *yan* means craving. Brought to America in the mid-nineteenth century it entered English slang as "yen yen" and eventually just "yen," which early in the twentieth century took the meaning of a craving for anything.

# ANIMALS

## Why is a theatrical flop called a "turkey"?

A "turkey" can describe any person or endeavour that doesn't live up to its promise, but is most commonly used to describe a bad play. In the late nineteenth century, the period between Thanksgiving and Christmas was the busiest season for the opening of new plays, just as it is now for movies. This hurried effort to catch the tourist trade served up disappointments with the same tedium as the turkey served for dinner between the two holidays, and so they were called turkeys.

## Why is the family non-achiever called a "black sheep"?

Most families have at least one embarrassing loafer who is referred to by the others, and sometimes by himself, as the "black sheep." A black sheep is considered worthless because, unlike the majority of sheep, its dark wool cannot be dyed. Although it takes as much time and nurturing to raise a black sheep as it does any other, its wool has very little market value, making raising it almost a waste of time to the shepherd.

## Why do you wish a pompous person would "get off his high horse"?

A person on a high horse is probably presuming to be more important than he truly is. In medieval times the height of your horse told of your rank in society and on the battlefield. Knights rode high on horses bred large and strong enough to bear the weight of the man and his armour. In ceremonial processions, kings and noblemen always rode the tallest horses, and anyone overstating his importance would be taken off his high horse.

## Why does "letting the cat out of the bag" prevent you from buying "a pig in a poke"?

A *poke* has the same origins as *pocket* and *pouch* and is a small bag within which a young pig could be packaged after being sold at a farmers' market. In 1540 it was recorded that unscrupulous farmers would sometimes replace the pig with a cat and advise purchasers not to open the bag until they reached home or the pig might escape. If the poke was opened, the cat was out of the bag, and the seller had been caught cheating.

## Why when someone's humiliated do we say they were forced to "eat crow"?

The expression "to eat crow" came from an incident during the War of 1812 when the Americans invaded Canada. A hungry New England soldier who strayed across enemy lines had shot a crow for food when he was discovered by an unarmed British officer who managed to get hold of the American's rifle by pretending to admire it. He then turned the weapon on the young man and forced him to eat part of the crow raw before letting him go.

## Why is something we consider untrue called a "cock and bull" story?

In the sixteenth century a papal *bull* or *bulla* was a decree from the Roman Catholic Pope and was sealed with a stamp bearing the likeness of St. Peter accompanied by the cock that crowed three times before the crucifixion. After the reformation, Martin Luther issued bulls of his own that contradicted the Vatican. His followers considered papal decrees as lies and referred to them from their seals as "cock and bull."

## Why is suddenly stopping a bad habit called "cold turkey"?

"Cold turkey" had the folk symbolism of stark circumstances without the trimmings (such as an unadorned sandwich made from the leftovers of a feast as a symbol of having seen better times) before it first appeared in print as a reference to drug withdrawal in 1921. The expression gained credence from the withdrawing addicts' desperate appearance — cold, pale, pimply skin, making them resemble a cold, uncooked turkey.

## Why is having an honest conversation referred to as "talking turkey"?

"Talking turkey" comes from an encounter between a white settler and a Native American in 1848. After they had bagged a turkey and a buzzard, the fast-talking white man suggested, "You can have the buzzard and I will take the turkey, or I will take the turkey and you can have the buzzard" — or, in modern language, "Heads I win, tails you lose." The Native's response, "Why don't you talk turkey with me?" was passed on so often by those overhearing the argument that talking turkey became part of the language.

## Why is the word *cuckold* used to describe the husband of an unfaithful wife?

*Cuckold* is a centuries-old metaphor for a deceived husband and is taken from the habits of the European cuckoo bird, which, in the spring, lays a single egg in the nest of some other bird to be hatched and then fed among its own chicks by the unsuspecting host. When a husband has been cuckolded, his nest has been violated by another, who might well have left behind his own offspring.

## Why when someone has done something crudely do we say they "rode roughshod" over the situation?

To ride roughshod over something means to have done something without regard or consideration for finesse or good manners. *Roughshod* refers to the once common practice of leaving the nails stuck out of a horses' shoes to keep the animal from slipping if it were going across country or through the bush. If roughshod horses passed over a garden or manicured lawn, the area would be torn up and completely destroyed.

## Why is a spelling competition called a "bee"?

Entire communities used to gather in a festive mood to build churches or to help neighbours building a barn or a home. These events were called "bees" because the number of people swarming around the task was similar to a busy hive of bees. The spelling bee is the lone survivor from this era and was the name used in 1925 by a Louisville newspaper for a national competition that is still going strong.

## Why is the ancestry of a Thoroughbred called its "pedigree"?

A pedigree is a lineage of heredity and must be traced to determine if a horse is a Thoroughbred, which is a direct descendant in the male line from three Arabian stallions brought to Britain and Ireland in the seventeenth and eighteenth centuries and bred with local mares. *Pedigree* came from the French *pie de grue*, meaning "the foot of a crane," which the forked lines of a family tree resemble.

## Why do we describe someone with deeply held beliefs as "dyed in the wool"?

"Dyed in the wool" describes someone whose thoughts on politics or religion just can't be changed. The original meaning of the phrase was applied to the dying of raw wool, which, if done in bulk before being combed or woven, holds its colour much longer than wool dyed after processing. Today, "dyed in the wool" means that like the colour in the unprocessed yarn, convictions ingrained early, during childhood, will last the longest.

## When creating or correcting something, why do we say we're "licking it into shape"?

When bear cubs are born, like many other newborn animals, they are covered by an amniotic membrane. To ancient people who observed the birth from a considerably safe distance, these cubs looked shapeless until their mothers would lick away the membrane to reveal the perfectly shaped body of the baby bear. Dating from Roman times, this belief gave us the expression for making something right by licking it into shape.

## Why when either humans or animals are on a rampage do we say they've "run amok"?

Running amok metaphorically means that someone is in some way dangerously out of control. An elephant that breaks free at a circus might also be described as running amok. *Amok* is a Malaysian word meaning "a state of murderous frenzy." Sixteenth-century explorers said that it was terrifying to see someone running amok, a condition brought on by drug use among some of the Malay.

# EXPRESSIONS

### Can a person be "on the level" if he's going "against the grain"?

Both "going against the grain" and being "on the level" are expressions from carpentry. When a bladed instrument is used to smooth a wooden surface it only works when applied with, or in the same direction as, the grain, otherwise it's a mess. A level ensures the precision of a frame alignment. Someone going against the grain is doing things wrong, and so is probably not as trustworthy as someone on the level.

### Why wouldn't you give a "tinker's dam" if you consider something useless?

A tinker travelled from town to town repairing tin pots, kettles, and pans and got his name from the noise he made while working. His equipment included clay from which he made a mould to hold melted solder for refastening handles and joints. He called this mould a "dam," and because it was only good for one pot, the tinker tossed it when the job was done. That's how a tinker's dam became synonymous with worthless.

### When we want someone to move faster why do we say, "Hurry up" instead of just "Hurry?"

The expression "hurry up" caught on during a time when most eating establishments had a dining room on the main floor and a kitchen in the basement. To hurry of course means to increase your pace, so "hurry up" became a specific order shouted by the headwaiter to speed the food up from the basement kitchen and into the dining room, where the phrase was heard so often by the patrons that it entered our language.

### Why do we say, "Buckle down" when it's time to get serious?

If a teacher or a foreman tells someone it's time to buckle down, they mean "Quit fooling around, this is serious business," and they're using an expression from the days of knighthood. When preparing for combat, knights required their squires to attend to their armour by oiling it, laying it out, and then buckling it onto their masters' bodies. How well this was done could be the difference between life and death for the knight, so buckling down was very serious business.

## Why do we say that a bad idea "won't hold water"?

The expression "won't hold water" comes from the legend of Tutia, a Roman Vestal Virgin who was accused of having lost her innocence. To prove herself not guilty she had to carry a sieve full of water from the Tiber River to the Temple of Vesta. If the sieve held the water she was innocent, but if not she would be buried alive. She passed the test and gave us the expression for failure, "It won't hold water."

## Why does a good punchline make a comedian "pleased as punch"?

Radio comedian Fred Allen once said that a good joke should have the same impact as a punch in the belly. The "punchline" is the twist that makes a joke funny, and the term was in use long before Fred Allen. It first appeared in *Variety* in 1921, but its use as the end of a skit goes back to the medieval husband and wife puppets Punch and Judy. Each skit ended with Punch getting the best of Judy, which gave us the expression "pleased as Punch."

## When we arrive at the last minute, why do we say we got there just in "the nick of time"?

The *nick* is a cut or notch made on a piece of wood; during medieval times, long before punch-in time clocks or other methods of modern tabulation, attendance, especially at schools and church services, was registered with a nick on a personalized stick of wood. If someone failed to show up on time, no nick was recorded, for which there would be suitable punishment.

## Why do we say that a timid person has "cold feet"?

To have cold feet means to lose your nerve when facing danger; it began meaning cowardly more than a hundred years ago. This is a bit harsh, because everyone's bodily extremities (including the hands and feet) become cold when terrified because under the circumstances, the body draws blood away from these areas to fuel vital organs for combat or flight. So cold feet don't make the coward ... it's the running away.

## Why, when wanting full speed and power, do we say, "Gun it" or "Pull out all the stops"?

"Gun it" comes from early aviation and auto mechanics, who coined the phrase as an instruction to get more speed by pulling out the full throttle. This sudden injection of fuel caused a minor explosion in the combustion engine, which sounded like the firing of a gun. Stops on a pipe organ control volume, so to pull out all the stops refers to accessing the organ's maximum power.

## Where did the expression "Mind your Ps and Qs" come from?

Mind your Ps and Qs means watch the details, and there are two popular explanations. The first is that because a lower case $p$ and $q$ are mirror images of each other, printing presses had to pay close attention to which one they used. The other, and more likely, explanation is that English pubs marked Ps and Qs on a blackboard to record each customer's consumption of pints and quarts. "Mind your Ps and Qs" meant keep an eye on your tab.

## Why do we call a critical instant the "moment of truth"?

The "moment of truth" is what the Spanish call that instant when a bullfighter chooses to make the final thrust of his sword and was introduced into English in Ernest Hemingway's 1932 novel *Death In The Afternoon*. The timing of that final move by the bullfighter is critical for both the matador and the animal, and so *el momento de la verdad*, or the moment of truth, became synonymous with any critical decision.

## If you want someone to stop "harping" on something why might you say, "Pipe down"?

The use of *harping*, as in repeating the same annoying statement or sound, comes from the repetitive and irritating noise made from tuning each string of a harp. If you tell the person harping on one string to "pipe down," you are using a naval term. On early naval vessels, the boatswain's final function for the day was to whistle or pipe down a signal for the crew to settle in and be quiet for the night.

## Why are the derelicts of "skid row" said to be "on the skids"?

To be "on the skids" means to be down on your luck and still falling. In the early twentieth century, skids were greased wooden runways used on dirt roads by the forest industry to make it easier to move logs from the bush to the river or the sawmill. The depressed street these skid roads passed through in a lumber town were lined by bars and flophouses where the transients looking for work lived, and so it was called "skid row."

## Where do we get the expression "toast of the town"?

By the eighteenth century, wealthy young men had turned feasting into an art, and at the core of the elaborate ritual was the drinking of wine. It was the custom to offer a toast to someone present with every new glass during dinner. When they tired of toasting themselves they would lift a glass in celebration of someone they might not even know, particularly a beautiful woman — who, if frequently admired this way, became known as the toast of the town.

## If you're being driven to "rack and ruin" where are you going?

Being driven to rack and ruin is sometimes expressed as "wreck and ruin," but either way you're in big trouble. *Rack* was the original reference and first appeared in the fifteenth century as a torture machine which encouraged victims to "rack their brains" to come up with the answers the inquisitors desired — otherwise they would be torn apart. So whether you're being driven to rack and ruin or wreck and ruin, unless you come up with the right answers, you're on your way to total destruction.

## What's the difference between "having your back to the wall" and "going to the wall"?

"Having your back to the wall" comes from street fighting and means you're in a desperate situation, and although there is no room to retreat you might still win if you fight off the attack with renewed energy. On the other hand, "going to the wall" means that although you are in an equally desperate situation, you are there willingly, even though there is no chance of winning. Going to the wall comes from the condemned facing a firing squad.

### Why do we say that someone indecisive is "on the fence"?

During the Revolutionary War, a prominent New Jersey jurist, Judge Imlay, hadn't yet committed to either the revolutionaries or the loyalists, so when Washington encountered one of Imlay's slaves he asked him which way the judge was leaning. Washington was so amused by the response that he retold it enough times for it to become part of our language. He said, "Until my master knows which is the strongest group, he's staying on the fence."

### Why, when embarking on a difficult project, does a group say they must "all hang together"?

The meaning of "all hanging together" is that our only hope is to combine our resources because we are already doomed as individuals. It's a quote from John Hancock, who was the first to step forward and sign the American Declaration of Independence. He said to those gathered, "We must all hang together; else we shall all hang separately," and the hanging he was referring to was death on the gallows for treason.

### Why do we say that something happened so quickly that it was over before you could say "Jack Robinson"?

Jack Robinson was a London social climber during the early eighteenth century. He made it his business to appear at as many gatherings as possible, where he would often present his card and have his name announced, then leave for the next function before meeting his hosts. This scandalous behavior made its way into a popular song, and eventually, "Before you could say Jack Robinson" meant any act of extreme haste.

**Why is a sudden surprise called a "bolt from the blue"?**

The word *bolt* has many uses, but all suggest surprising quickness and all originated as a reference to an arrow from a crossbow. The word *thunderbolt* for lightning first appeared in the sixteenth century, while *blue* as a description of a clear sky appeared about a hundred years later. Since nothing could be more surprising than lightning from a cloudless sky, a "bolt from the blue" entered the language as a description of a sudden and unexpected event.

**Why is a false promise called "pie in the sky"?**

In the early 1900s, a radical workers' union used a song called *The Preacher and the Slave* to blame the church for suppressing the poor with promises of rewards in heaven. The song included these lines (and from them, "pie in the sky" took the meaning of a false promise):

> You will eat, by and by,
> In that glorious land above the sky.
> Work and pray, live on hay,
> You'll get pie in the sky when you die, by and by.

**Why is a notable achievement said to be a "feather in your cap"?**

Among tribal warriors, including those native to North America, a feather was awarded for each enemy killed in combat. These were worn as a headdress and eventually on armoured helmets; like today's campaign medals, the most decorated warriors stood out as heroes. Women began wearing feathers in their caps as a signal of betrothal after it became customary for a knight to give one of his hard-earned feathers to the woman he loved.

## What does it mean to be at someone's "beck and call"?

To be at someone's "beck and call" means to be standing by and prepared to immediately respond to that person's needs. The expression comes from the rules of servitude, when a *beck* was a silent signal, such as a nod of the head or a hand gesture, used to summon a servant. If this subtlety didn't work, then the master or mistress would resort to a *call*. This meant they had used a beck and a call to get the domestic's attention.

## Why when we memorize something do we say, "I know it by heart"?

Saying that we have learned something "by heart" means, of course, that we have committed it to memory, which more than likely involved a process of repetition, called learning by rote. *Rote* is from *rota*, the Latin word for wheel, meaning that to memorize something we turn it over in our minds many times before knowing it by heart. The ancient Greeks believed that it was the heart, and not the brain, where thoughts were held.

## Why do we say that something complete "fills" or "fits the bill"?

If something "fills" or "fits the bill," it's satisfying, whether it's a good meal or a job well done. The expressions come from the days when theatrical advertising was done through handbills or posters. "Filling the bill" meant adding acts to pad a weak program, but if a single star could pull in an audience through his or her individual fame and talent, their name was all that was needed so it was enlarged to fit the bill.

## Where did the expression "neck of the woods" come from?

Today, "this neck of the woods" would mean this specific neighbourhood. The phrase comes from the very beginning of European settlement in North America. It's from the Anglo adaptation of the Algonquin Indian word *naiak*, meaning a narrow strip or corner of wooded land, usually protruding into water. The Algonquin *naiak* was interpreted by white settlers as *neck*, and became neck of the woods.

## Why is unexpected trouble called "getting into a scrape"?

"Getting into a scrape" means to be in a difficult situation and is as old as England itself. When that country was a primeval forest, it was overrun with wild deer. To avoid hunters, these deer would use their sharp hooves to scrape deep gullies into the ground, where they would huddle for cover. In time these would become overgrown and difficult to detect, so while out in the forest it wasn't uncommon to fall into a scrape.

## When someone's making inappropriate fun why do we say, "Quit joshing around"?

*Joshing* means joking or kidding around, usually at someone else's expense. It comes from the writings of the great American humourist Josh Billings, whose caustic humour took on the establishment big shots during the nineteenth century. As America's first best-selling author, he was so widely read that his name became synonymous with deflating pompous egos and so, to josh someone took on the meaning "to make fun of."

## Why when challenging the unknown do we say, "Let her rip"?

"Let her rip" is an expression we use when we are apprehensive about the outcome of a new venture but determined to see what happens. Its origin is the tombstone inscription R.I.P for "rest in peace," and the phrase came into use as a pun for embarking on a new and unknown adventure because to the religious people who coined it, although whatever comes after death isn't a certainty, we have no choice but to just do it.

### Why do we say that something dwindling is "petering out"?

Supplies that are gradually diminishing are said to be "petering out," and someone exhausted is "all petered out." The expression was used by both Abraham Lincoln and Mark Twain and is derived from a very old mining term used to describe a vein of ore that splits into branches and then gradually runs out, leaving the miners and investors high and dry. The image is of Saint Peter, who left Jesus when he was needed most.

### Why do we say something perfect is right "on the nose"?

"On the nose" didn't come from horse racing, it came from radio. Several common hand gestures came from the early days of radio broadcasting, when elaborate productions required the director in the studio to be able to communicate without speech, and so they used hand signals. For "cut" a forefinger was slashed across the throat. Holding up the forefinger touching the thumb meant "good performance," and touching the nose signalled "perfect timing." It was right on the nose.

### Why is the use of behind the scenes influence called "pulling strings"?

Marionettes are puppets controlled by strings and were popular at the courts of the French monarchy. The puppet shows satirized gossip and could be embarrassing to anyone involved in scandal. When money was slipped to the puppeteer to keep him quiet, or to influence him to embarrass someone else, it was said that the person offering the bribe — and not the puppeteer — was the one pulling the strings of the marionette.

**What ends are we talking about when we say we are trying to "make ends meet"?**

"Making ends meet" means to balance what you make with what is required to live, especially in difficult times, and comes to us from the sixteenth-century farmers of England. The saying refers to the beginning and the end of a year — or from the end of one year to the end of the next. If someone could overcome the unpredictable and seasonal problems throughout the year without losing money, they had survived by making ends meet.

**What's the origin of the expressions "rough and ready" and "rough and tumble"?**

Both "rough and ready" and "rough and tumble" are expressions that came from the sport of boxing. *Rough* still means "crude," so "rough and ready" meant a semi-pro or amateur who, although unpolished and perhaps not as well trained as he should be, was still considered good enough to enter the ring. If a contest was "rough and tumble," both fighters had agreed to throw away the rules, which led to a lot of tumbling.

**Why is something ordinary said to be "run of the mill"?**

Since the dawn of the industrial age, anything that is unspectacular yet functional has been called "run of the mill." When a raw product is to be mechanically processed, whether through a gristmill or the mill of a mine, it emerges in bulk before the different sizes and qualities have been separated by value. Worth can't be determined until further refining and so everything looks the same — and that's why anything ordinary is called run of the mill.

**Why do we say that someone lost is going from "pillar to post"?**

Going from "pillar to post" means moving from one bad situation to another. The expression comes from the Puritans of New England, who punished those who strayed from their strict moral code by taking them to the pillory where, in public view, their hands and feet were tied until they repented. If they refused to repent, they were taken to a whipping post and flogged until they acknowledged their sins ... Thus, they had gone from pillar to post.

**Where did the expression as "drunk as blazes" come from?**

To be drunk as blazes comes from a feast day created by the Orthodox church to honour a sainted Armenian bishop named Blais who was beheaded by the Roman Emperor Licinius for refusing to deny his faith in 316 A.D. The excessive drinking on St. Blais's day caused the revellers to be referred to as "drunken Blaisers," and soon anyone anywhere who was overly intoxicated was said to be as drunk as blazes.

**Why is a jilted person said to have been "left in the lurch"?**

To be left in the lurch means to have been put in an embarrassing or difficult position; it is most commonly used when either a bride or groom fails to show up for a wedding. *Lurch* was originally spelled *lurche* and was the name of a card game now known as cribbage. The first player to score sixty-one won the round, and if this was accomplished before an opponent scored thirty, the loser was said to have been "lurched," or left so far behind they had no chance of winning.

**Why do we say that people who have overcome the odds have "pulled themselves up by their own bootstraps"?**

In the sixteenth century, bootstraps were leather loops sewn into the top, sides, or back of high-fitting boots. These were so difficult to put on that it required the help of a device with a handle and a hook and required so much energy that the vivid image of people lifting themselves up during the process — although impossible — became a figure of speech for accomplishing what appeared to be unachievable.

## Why is the person with the least significance called the "low man on the totem pole"?

First Nations tribes told their history through the elaborate carvings of creatures on tall totem poles, but the idea that the bottom image was the least important is wrong. It originated with comedian Fred Allen, who, in 1941, wrote, "If humorist H. Allen Smith were an Indian he'd be low man on the totem pole." Smith later used the phrase as a book title, and the expression caught on.

## Why might you say that someone irrational is "mad as a hatter"?

Years ago, manufacturers of felt hats used mercury to treat the wool, which made it easier to pound the fibres into felt. Mercury poisoning attacks the nervous system, which caused many hatters to develop tremors and then madness. In Alice's Wonderland tea party, she met not only a Mad Hatter but also another descriptive expression, "mad as a March hare." The hare breeds during March, so he might be excused for his absurd antics.

## What does it mean to say that you wouldn't give "one iota" for something?

If someone doesn't care one iota, they don't care very much. Like the letter "i" in English, an iota is the ninth and smallest letter of the Greek alphabet, and because the English letters "I" and "J" were often confused, *iota* became *jot*, with both words meaning something very small. That's why to "jot something down" means to condense information, while an iota is just a little bit more than a tittle, which is the dot over the "i."

### Why do we say that something deteriorating is either "going" or "gone to pot"?

If a relationship or a career is going to pot, it means its glory days are over. The expression originated in 1542, long before refrigeration, and came from the urgency to save leftovers from a substantial meal before they went bad. As a metaphor, "going to pot" means that like the leftovers from a great meal, circumstances now assign the subject to something more humble, like a stew.

### Why does "back to square one" mean starting over?

During the 1930s, the BBC broadcast soccer, or football, games on the radio. As an aid to listeners they published a map of the playing field, which was divided into numbered squares. The commentators would mention the square number of the action after each description of the play. Square one was near the goaltender, so that to score you needed to carry the play the full length of the field.

### Why when someone's been dispatched do we say they've been "snuffed out"?

Snuff, of course, is a pulverized tobacco that is inhaled through the nostrils. During the eighteenth century in Ireland, it was a common custom to place a dish of snuff inside the coffin so that those at the wake could enjoy a pinch while they said their final farewell. One woman loved the tobacco smell so much that she had her coffin filled with snuff and two bushels distributed among the guests. This custom gave us the expression "snuffed out."

## What's the difference between "marking time" and "killing time"?

"Marking time" is a military command for soldiers in close-order drill to stop their forward progress but to keep their feet moving in precision so they can quickly resume marching on command. Marking time means that although your progress has been temporarily stopped you are fully prepared to continue when the time is right. On the other hand, "killing time" means that you're doing absolutely nothing, or, as the proverb says, "You don't kill time, time kills you."

## Why do we say a simple procedure is "cut and dried" unless we "hit a snag"?

"Cut and dried" means it's a finished job and comes from the lumber industry. The two processes for preparing wood for sale are to cut it and then dry it. The same industry gave us the expression "hit a snag," meaning we've got a problem. A *snag* is a tree trunk stuck on the river bottom with one end protruding just enough to slow or stop the log drive, which can't continue until the snag is removed.

## Why is "forty winks" used as a synonym for napping?

In 1571 the Church of England introduced thirty-nine articles which clergymen of the church were required to accept before their ordination. An 1872 publication of the British humour magazine *Punch* suggested that reading these catechisms was tedious and that their meaning could be missed: "If a man, after reading through the thirty-nine articles were to take forty winks ..." From this point on, "forty winks" has meant a brief nap.

### Why do we say we're "in stitches" when we laugh hard?

Like the stitches in sewing, those in the side from both running and laughing all come from the verb *stick*. The expression "to stick someone" is over a thousand years old and means "to stab" or "to prod." The stabbing or sticking of a needle through cloth in sewing is thus called a stitch, and because both the pain in the side from running and that from laughing feels like you've been stabbed or stuck with something, these too are called stitches.

### What does a handkerchief have to do with "wearing your heart on your sleeve"?

When fifteenth-century French sailors brought back linen head coverings worn by Chinese field workers as protection from the sun, they called them *couvrechef*, or "head covering," which when Anglicized became *kerchief*. Because they were carried in the hand, they became hand kerchiefs. Women began giving scented handkerchiefs to suitors, which the suitors then tucked under their sleeves in a ritual known as wearing his heart on his sleeve.

### Why is a dirty story said to be "off colour"?

In Britain, "off colour" has always indicated that someone might feel under the weather because the colour of their skin has changed from its normal hue to pale. In America the expression "off colour" has a related but different meaning. When someone says something that is considered sexually shocking or impolite, it will often cause those listening to blush from a rush of blood that changes their skin colour to red, so the story that caused the skin colour change is referred to as being off colour.

### Why is challenging the odds called playing "fast and loose"?

"Fast and loose" was a medieval street game played by tricksters in much the same way as a shell game is played today. A coiled belt was laid out on a table with what appeared to be a knotted loop in the centre. Then a mark was invited to stab a knife in the loop, sticking it "fast" to the table. When the huckster easily lifted the belt the sucker lost his money for falling for the illusion that he had made the belt fast instead of leaving it loose.

## How did "one fell swoop" come to mean a single decisive action?

The expression "one fell swoop" was introduced by Shakespeare in *Macbeth*. When Macduff learns that his wife and children have been murdered he exclaims: "What, all my pretty chickens and their dam / At one fell swoop?" Metaphorically, Macduff compares his wife and children to chickens and their murderer to a bird of prey. During Shakespeare's time, *fell* meant "fierce," and survives today in the word *felon*.

# PROVERBS

# PROVERBS

## What was the original meaning of "variety is the spice of life"?

When William Cowper wrote, "Variety's the very spice of life" in 1785, he was reflecting on the ever-changing fashion of clothes. The idea had been first expressed by ancient writers in different ways, but it was the genius of Cowper that caused "variety is the spice of life" to become an English proverb. Other common Cowper idioms include "The worse for wear" and "God moves in mysterious ways."

## When facing disaster why do we say someone is "between the Devil and the deep blue sea"?

To be "between the Devil and the deep blue sea" has largely been replaced by being "between a rock and a hard place," which came out of Arizona and originally meant to be bankrupt. The Devil is the seam of a sailing ship's hull, which was reinforced to support cannons and was where a board was fastened for those forced to walk the plank. The condemned sailor couldn't turn back, so his only option was the deep blue sea.

## Why do we say a hypocrite is a "pot calling the kettle black"?

"The pot calling the kettle black" first entered a dictionary in 1699 with the explanation, "When one accuses another of what he is as deep in himself." When kitchen stoves were fired by wood and coal, both the kettle and the pot would become black through time, so both were equally tarnished. Another explanation is that because both were made of copper, the more prized kettle might have been polished, which would offer the grungy pot a reflection of himself.

## Why do we say "Every cloud has a silver lining"?

"Every cloud has a silver lining" originated in a poem written in 1634 by John Milton. Milton tells of a young woman who becomes lost and alone in the woods after being separated from her two brothers. As night falls, her terror is lifted and her prayers answered when she sees a dark cloud turn its bright side down to guide her and says: "There does a sable cloud turn forth her Silver Lining on the night."

## When something valuable is destroyed while eliminating waste, why do we say they've "thrown the baby out with the bathwater"?

During the time when the entire family, beginning with the eldest, used the same bathwater, you had to be careful that a child wasn't still inside when it came time to throw out the dirty water. But the phrase was introduced in 1909 by George Bernard Shaw, who wrote, "Like all reactionaries, he usually empties the baby out with the bathwater."

**What is the real meaning of the proverb, "A friend in need, is a friend indeed"?**

A friend in need could be someone in trouble who needs your help and indeed becomes your friend in order to get it, but it's usually interpreted as meaning a friend who stands with you during a difficult time. But if you accept that "in deed" is two words instead of one, it extends the definition of a good friend from one who stands with you to one who actually helps solve the problem.

**What is the origin of the phrase, "It matters not whether you win or lose, but how you play the game"?**

The noble expression about how you play the game is a Greek historian's fifth-century B.C. reference to the Olympians. He wrote, "Tis not for Money they contend, but for Glory". It resurfaced in 1927 when the great sportswriter Grantland Rice wrote, "For when the great scorer comes to write against your name, He marks not that you won or lost but how you played the game."

# SONGS, POEMS & NURSERY RHYMES

## Who was Humpty Dumpty?

The nursery rhyme in which "Humpty Dumpty has a great fall" dates back to 1493 and refers to King Richard III of England. Richard had a hump on his back and had been dumped by his mount in the thick of battle when he cried, "My kingdom for a horse" before being slain. The last line, "Couldn't put Humpty together again," was originally "Couldn't put Humpty up again," meaning back on his horse.

## Who is Mary in the nursery rhyme "Mary, Mary, quite contrary"?

The children's nursery rhyme "Mary, Mary, quite contrary" is about Mary, Queen of Scots, and emerged during her struggle for power with Queen Elizabeth I. The "pretty maids all in a row" were her ladies in waiting (the Marys: Seaton, Fleming, Livingston, and Beaton). The cockleshells were decorations on an elaborate gown given to her by the French Dauphin. The rhyme was popular when Mary was beheaded in 1587.

## What is the origin of Mother Goose's nursery rhymes?

Most nursery rhymes were never intended for children. For centuries, these ballads came from bawdy folk songs or spoofs on social issues of the day, often sung or recited as limericks in local taverns. "Nursery" wasn't used to describe them until efforts were made in the nineteenth century to clean them up as children's lullabies. In 1697, a French writer, Charles Perrault, published *Tales of My Mother Goose*, a collection of fairy tales (including "Little Red Riding Hood" and "Puss in Boots").

**Why did Yankee Doodle stick a feather in his cap and call it macaroni?**

The famous American patriotic song "Yankee Doodle" actually began as an English song of derision against the colonists. At the time there was a Macaroni Club in London which catered to foppish, wealthy young men who copied everything Italian, including sticking a feather in their caps, which to many became the sign of a "sissy." When the Americans began winning the war they took possession of the song "Yankee Doodle" as revenge.

**In the Scottish song "Loch Lomond," what's the difference between the high and the low roads?**

In the song "Loch Lomond," two wounded Scottish soldiers are in a foreign prison. One will be set free, but the one speaking is to be executed. When he says, "You take the high road and I'll take the low road," he's referring to the Celtic belief that if a man dies in a foreign land, the fairies will guide his spirit home along the "low road," while the living man will travel an earthly or "high road" that will take longer.

**Where did the Do, Re, Mi vocal music scale come from?**

In the tenth century, Guido d' Arezzo was having trouble teaching monks their Gregorian chants, so he replaced the A, B, C music scale with sound symbols which we now know as Do, Re, Mi. He could point to a spot where he had written them on his hand and the monks would know exactly which note to sing. These hand symbols evolved into the phonetic music scale and gave Maria a song to sing in *The Sound of Music*.

**Al Jolson sang about it, and Stephen Foster and Ira Gershwin wrote popular songs about it ... so where is the Swanee River?**

In the first draft of his 1851 song "The Old Folks At Home," Stephen Foster's river was the Pedee, but that didn't work so he searched an atlas and found the Suwannee River, which he shortened to Swanee. In 1919, Gershwin and Irving Caesar reused the name in the Jolson classic and made the Swanee the most famous river that never existed.

# LAW & FINANCE

**Why do we have piggy banks instead of bunny banks or kitty banks?**

In medieval England, pots and dishes were made from a clay known as "pygg," and it was common practice to save spare change in a kitchen pot. Around 1600, an English potter who was unfamiliar with this custom was asked to make a pygg bank, which he misunderstood to be a clay vessel in the shape of the animal; the end result was a clay pig with a slot in its back. The piggy bank had arrived.

**Why is a charge on imports and exports called a "tariff"?**

When the Arab Moors invaded Spain in the eighth century they brought with them profound cultural and creative concepts that influence that country to this day. For example, when the matador skirts the bull in their life and death ballet, the Spanish crowd cries *ole*, which evolved from the Arabic word *Allah*. Twenty miles from Gibraltar is the seaport of Tarifa, where the Moors introduced bounties on ships entering the Mediterranean, leaving us the word *tariff*.

## What is the origin of the dollar sign?

Thomas Jefferson used the letter "S" with two lines through it to symbolize a dollar in a document within which he suggested the dollar as the primary unit of American currency in 1784. Prior to this the symbol was in use for the peso throughout Latin America. Consequently, the most widely accepted explanation is that the dollar sign ($) is a depiction of the twin pillars of Hercules wrapped with a scroll, as found on early Spanish pieces of eight.

## Why do we say someone without money is both "broke" and "bankrupt"?

*Bank* comes from the Italian word *banca*, meaning "bench," over which medieval moneylenders did business in the streets of Venice. If he became insolvent, the law intervened and broke the lender's bench, which in Italian is *banca rotta*. *Rotta* referred to the broken bench, but another figurative word in use for a broken man was the Latin *ruptus*. With his bench broken, the banker's spirit was *banca ruptus*.

## Why do we say they'll "foot the bill" when someone's paying all the costs?

To foot the bill dates back to a period when women had no means of financial support, so families offered dowries to entice eligible men to marry their daughters. The cost of the wedding and the dowry were "footed up," meaning itemized, then totalled at the bottom of the ledger. In the fifteenth century, the "foot" was the bottom line, so to foot the bill meant to pay the full amount at the bottom of the invoice.

## What is the legal origin of the grandfather clause?

The term "grandfather clause" means something is exempt if in practice before a new law forbids it, and comes from a legal trick used by the Southern States to keep former slaves from voting. A law was introduced requiring the passing of a literacy test before anyone, black or white, could vote. The only exemptions were people whose grandfathers had voted prior to the new law. This gave all whites the right to vote, and virtually all blacks were disqualified.

## Why do we call a way out of a legal obligation a "loophole"?

Loops were originally holes in the thick stone walls of a medieval fortress. Some of these holes were small and used for observation. Others were slits that widened on the inside, enabling an archer to safely shoot out arrows during a siege. Finally, these walls had larger, hidden loops or openings through which it was possible to escape during a losing battle. These escape "loopholes" gave us the modern meaning.

## Why is a change described as "a whole new ball of wax"?

Seventeenth-century English law used a unique way to settle the contested division of an estate. The executor divided the estate into the number of heirs, then wrote down each parcel of land in the estate on an individual scrawl. To keep it secret, each scrawl was then covered by wax and made into a ball, which was then placed into a hat. Beginning with the eldest, the heirs then drew the balls at random, with the estate settled by the contents of each ball of wax.

## Why do we say that someone in serious trouble is "in hot water"?

Before there were trials by jury, there were trials by ordeal. The ordeal depended on the crime, but if it carried the death penalty the accused could find himself in hot water. The defendant was forced into a large cauldron of boiling water, and if he survived he was clearly innocent, but on the other hand if he died he must have committed the crime because the Supreme Being hadn't interfered.

## Why when there is no doubt of someone's guilt do we say they were caught "red-handed"?

*Redhand* goes back to the fifteenth century Scottish people and became "red-handed" within judicial circles in Britain during the eighteenth century. It means that someone has been caught in the act of committing a crime or that there is an irrefutable body of evidence to establish the criminal's guilt. Its original reference was to murder, and the red on the hands of the accused was the blood of his victim.

## How did the terms of divorce evolve?

Divorce to the Athenians and Romans was allowed whenever a man's like turned to dislike. In the seventh century it was recorded that Anglo-Saxon men could divorce a wife who was barren, rude, oversexed, silly, habitually drunk, overweight, or quarrelsome. Throughout history, in societies where men were paid dowries, divorce favoured the husband; however, in matrilineal societies where the woman was esteemed, mutual consent was required. The word *alimony* means "nourishment."

## Why do we say that someone who's been through hard times has been "through the mill"?

The expression "through the mill" has nothing to do with a grist or paper mill. It came from legal circles, and in the commercial world it means to have been through bankruptcy. The phrase comes from the original English court, where petitions for discharge of debt due to insolvency were first heard. This special court was called the Mill.

To have been through the mill now means to have gone through any hard time, including bankruptcy.

## Why are pedestrians who break the law called "jaywalkers"?

When cars were introduced, crossing city streets became a lot more hazardous than when horse-drawn carriages were the only traffic. New safety laws were introduced, and anyone ignoring them was considered a country bumpkin. In the early part of the twentieth century, unsophisticated rural people were often referred to as "jays," as in just another bird from the country, and so their ignorance about how to properly cross a street became known as jaywalking.

## Why, when someone avoids a punishment or obligation, do we say that they got off "scot-free"?

The *scot* in "scot-free" has nothing to do with Scotsmen; as a matter of fact, the archaic word *scot* was borrowed from the Norse and meant a contribution of tax or treasure. Used in its present sense, *scot* first appeared in English in the thirteenth century, and its use with *free* became common in the sixteenth century. To be scot-free meant then, as it does now, "to be free from payment or obligation as well as punishment."

## Why is a criminal record called a "rap sheet"?

*Rap* surfaced as a word imitating sound in the fourteenth century. Among other things, it perfectly describes the noise made by someone knocking, or "rapping," at the door. In the criminal sense it's the rap of a judge's gavel sounding the end of a trial that gave us such phrases as "a bad rap" and "a bum rap." A rap sheet is a record of criminal charges wherein the suspect couldn't prove his innocence before the rap of the gavel.

TRIVIA

## Why do we call gossip or unimportant information "trivia"?

The Romans were well-known for their road building, and from their Latin noun *trivium*, meaning a place where three roads meet, there derived a word for insignificant information. At a three-road intersection, traffic would slow and congest, offering a great chance for light gossip and meaningless conversation. So from *tri*, meaning "three," and *via*, meaning "roadway," the Romans gave us *trivia*, a word for useless information.

## What does it mean to have your "mojo" working?

*Mojo* is a word from the black Creole culture of the coastal regions of South Carolina and Georgia and probably arrived in some form with the slaves from Africa. It means "magic," and although it's had minor sub-cultural use as a jazz reference to drugs and sex, a mojo is a good luck charm enhanced through voodoo with the ability to cast a positive spell. If you've got your mojo working, then everything's going your way.

## Where did the pharmacist's symbol of "Rx" come from?

To the Romans, the pursuit of the healing arts and the distribution of medicine was the highest professional calling possible and therefore could only be ordained by Jupiter. The "R" in "Rx" is from the Latin word *recipere*, meaning "to have been prescribed" or "to take," while the small "x" was the god king's symbol of approval. To the Romans, the "Rx" meant that the great god Jupiter himself had a hand in the prescription.

## How did the seven days of the week get their names?

Although originating in Roman mythology, many of our names for days of the week came from the Vikings.
"Sunday" is a tribute to the sun.

"Monday" is a tribute to the moon.
"Tuesday" is from the Germanic war god Tiu.
"Wednesday" takes its name from the Germanic sky god Woden.
"Thursday" is from the Norse thunder god Thor.
"Friday" is from the Norse love goddess Frigg.
"Saturday" is named after the Roman god Saturn.

## Why do Americans pronounce the last letter of the alphabet "zee" while Canadians say "zed"?

The last letter of our alphabet is from the Greek word *zeta*, which in standard English became *zed*. There were, however, parts of Britain that shortened *zed* to *zee*, and it was from these regions that many people immigrated to the United States. Canada's first immigrants (including the French) were all from regions that used the "zed" pronunciation. In 1828, Webster's first dictionary favoured "zee" as a distinct American sound.

## Could an Irishman go to a "shindig" and take on the whole "shebang" with his "shillelagh"?

A shindig, a shebang, and a shillelagh are all from Irish expressions. *Shindig* comes from the fighting Irishman's habit of digging the steel toe of his boot into his opponent's shins. *Shebang* is from *shebeen,* an Irish reference to an illegal bootlegger. His wooden club took its name from the famous oak trees near the Irish town of Shillelagh — so yes, he could go to a shindig and wipe out the whole shebang with his shillelagh.

## How are the two Presidents Bush related to President Franklin Delano Roosevelt?

George Herbert Walker Bush became the second descendant of passengers on the *Mayflower* to become president; his son George W. Bush was the third. In 1620, Jane De La Noye was a small girl who arrived in America with her parents aboard the *Mayflower*. She was the first president Bush's grandmother eleven times removed. Her cousin, Phillip De La Noye, had his name Americanized to Delano, and his grandson eleven times removed was Franklin Delano Roosevelt, making he and the two George Bushes cousins.

## We all know what a "YUPPIE" is, but what are a "TAFFIE," a "DINK," and a "DROPPIE"?

YUPPIES are Young Urban Professional People. The U.S. Census Bureau has created many other acronyms to identify other social groups. TAFFIES are Technologically Advanced Families who are wired to the Internet. DINK stands for Dual Income No Kids, while DROPPIES is from the first letters of Disillusioned, Relatively Ordinary Professionals Preferring Independent Employment Situations.

## What is a Catch-22?

A Catch-22 is an impossible situation. In Joseph Heller's 1961 novel *Catch-22*, the protagonist tries every means possible to avoid flying dangerous missions in order to survive the war. The problem was Catch-22, a regulation that specified that if a man was afraid to fly then he was sane and had to, but if he flew he was crazy and didn't have to. Either way, at some point he had to fly.

## Why do we call the end of the day "evening," and why is it divided into "twilight" and "dusk"?

*Twilight* is defined by the ancient word *twi*, which means "half" or "between," so twilight is the time between light and darkness. *Dusk* is the final stage of twilight and is from the lost English word *dox*, which meant "dark" or "darker." *Evening* comes from the ancient word *aefen*, meaning "late," and came to mean the general time between sunset and when you went to sleep.

## Do only the most intelligent graduate from university?

A proper education is an advantage to any mind, but intelligence doesn't guarantee a formal education. Albert Einstein left school at fifteen after his teacher described him as "retarded"; Thomas Edison dropped out at eight. Up to 50 percent of North Americans born with a genius IQ never graduate high school. They can take comfort in these words from Emerson: "I pay the school master, but it's the schoolboys who educate my son."

## How long is a moment, and what is the precise time of a jiffy?

When we use *moment* or *jiffy*, as in "I'll be back in a moment" or "She'll be with you in a jiffy," we usually mean in an undefined but brief period of time — but in fact, both have a precise length. Although lost through time, a moment was originally an English reference for ninety seconds, while a jiffy is from science and is one one-hundredth of a second, the time it takes light in a vacuum to travel one centimetre.

## Why do so many Scottish and Irish surnames begin with "Mac" as in MacDonald, and "O" as in O'Connor?

One of the ancient Celtic traditions of Scotland and Ireland was (in much the same manner as for American slaves) that all the serfs who worked his land used the name of the clan chieftain. In Gaelic, the prefix *Mac* means "son," while O means "grandson" or "descendant of." Both were used to keep track of the true bloodline. MacDonald means "the son of Donald," while O'Connor means "the grandson of Connor."

## Why are precious stones such as diamonds weighed in carats?

The word *carat* comes from the carob bean, which grows on the *cerantonia siliqua* tree. Each bean is so remarkably near the same size and weight that the ancients used it as a universal measurement for precious stones. There are approximately 142 carob beans, or carats, to the ounce. Each carat is divided into one hundred points, individually weighing about the same as three bread crumbs.

## What is the difference between a settee, a divan, and a couch?

A settee, a divan, and a couch are all parlour furniture designed for sitting. *Settee* entered the language from the German *setlaz*, which means simply "seat." *Divan* is from the Persian word for "council of rulers" and was given as a name to an armless couch. The word *couch* originally referred to a bed and comes from the French word *coucher*, meaning "to lie in place" … like "Voulez-vous coucher avec moi."

## What does the Statue of Liberty have to do with the word *gadget*?

The word *gadget* first appeared in 1886, the year the French gave America the Statue of Liberty. That same year, a man named Gaget, one of the partners in the French company that had built the Liberty, conceived the idea of creating miniature statues to sell to Americans in Paris as souvenirs. The Americans mispronounced "Gaget" and called their miniature Libertys "gadgets," and a new word for something small was born.

## What is the origin of the polka dot?

The polka dot is a leftover from the polka dance craze that was introduced to America in 1835. *Polka* is the Polish word for "Polish woman," but the dance came from Czechoslovakia — just like the song "American Woman" came from Canada. The dance was in vogue up until the end of the nineteenth century, during which time dozens of by-products capitalized on its popularity, including one that still lingers: wearing apparel with the polka dot pattern.

## Is there a difference between a penknife and a jackknife?

The original difference between a jackknife and a penknife was size. Both had blades that folded into the handle for safety. The small penknife came first and was carried in a pocket in a sheath and was used for making or repairing quill pens. *Pen* is derived from *penna*, the Latin word meaning "feather." The jackknife was simply a large, all-purpose penknife, so called because it was a handy tool for sailors, who, at the time, were called "Jacks."

## Why do the hands of a clock move to the right?

Early mechanical timepieces didn't have hands. They signalled time with bells. Then one hand was introduced, indicating the hour only, until eventually sophisticated mechanics introduced the more precise minute and then second hands. Because clocks were invented in the northern hemisphere, the hands followed the same direction as the shadows on a sundial. If they'd been invented in the southern hemisphere, "clockwise" would be in the opposite direction.

## Why is a hospital's emergency selection process called "triage"?

*Triage* is from the French *trier*, meaning to compare and select, and was used in reference to sorting livestock for culling or slaughter. Triage entered medicine during the First World War, when battlefield physicians were overwhelmed with the wounded and dying. The least likely to live were treated last. In modern hospitals the order of triage is reversed, with priority given to the most seriously in need,

## Why is every fourth year called a "leap year"?

A leap year has 366 days, with an extra day added to February. Every year divisible by four is a leap year except those completing a century, which must be divisible by four hundred. It's called a leap year because normally the date that falls on a Monday this year will fall on Tuesday next year and then Wednesday the year after that. In the fourth year it will "leap" over Thursday and fall on Friday.

## What is the rule of thumb?

In 1976, NOW incorrectly linked the expression "rule of thumb" with a 1782 public statement by an English judge that in his opinion, a man should have the right to beat his wife as long as the stick used was no thicker than his thumb. In fact, the real "rule of thumb" is a reference to building or baking something through the knowledge of experience rather than precise science, with the thumb being an instrument for a rough and improvised measurement.

## Why is a complete list of letters named the "alphabet," and why is a river mouth called a "delta"?

One of the first things we learn in school is our ABCs, a list of all letters used in the English language. The name comes from the first two letters in the original Greek alphabet, alpha and beta. The triangular mouth of the Nile River was called a "delta" because, like all rivers leading into the sea, it's shaped like the fourth Greek letter. Every delta in the world took its name from the Nile.

**What part did the Big Dipper play in naming the frozen north the Arctic?**

As part of the constellation of Ursa Major, the Big Dipper can be seen the entire year throughout Europe and most of North America, and it becomes brighter as you travel north. The Romans followed the Greeks in naming the seven-star constellation containing the Big Dipper "the Bear," which in Latin is *ursa*. In Greek the word for bear is *arktos*, which gave us the name Arctic for the northern land beneath the Bear.

**What's the difference between a spider's web and a cobweb?**

All spiders create their webs through a liquid secretion that hardens in the air. These webs are nearly invisible, especially to the insects they trap. In modern language, the spider's web becomes a cobweb only after it collects dust and becomes visible, so the webs are different in name only. The word *cob* came from writings as early as the thirteenth century and had evolved from *coppe*, an early word for spider.

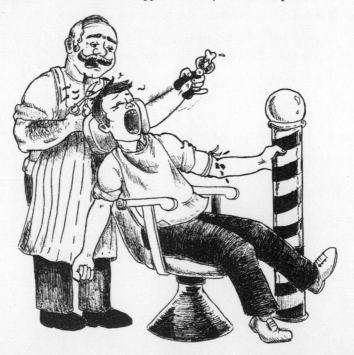

## What is the origin of the red and white barber pole?

The Roman word for beard is *barba*, which gave us the term *barber*. Early barbers cut hair and trimmed beards, but they also pulled teeth and practiced medicinal bloodletting. This last procedure required the patient to expose his veins by squeezing a pole painted red to hide the bloodstains. When not in use the red pole was displayed outside wrapped in the white gauze used as bandages, and it eventually became the official trademark of the barber.

## Why is the common winter viral infection called the "flu"?

In 1743, an outbreak of a deadly cold-like fever originated in Italy and swept through Europe. Because doctors believed that diseases and epidemics were ordained or influenced by the stars they called it (as the press reported it from Italy) an *influenza*. The English word for influenza is *influence*, which although abbreviated to *flu* still means the disease flows from the influence of the heavens.

# QUESTION LIST

## Customs

## Food & Drink

## People & Places

## Pop Culture

## Entertainment & Leisure

## Sports

## Politics & the Military

## Ships & Sailing

## Holidays

## Beliefs & Superstitions

## Words

## Animals

## Expressions

**Proverbs**

## Trivia